in their own words

blur

GW00472689

Mick St. Michael

OMNIBUS PRESS
LONDON · NEW YORK · SYDNEY

Copyright © 1996 Omnibus Press
(A Division of Book Sales Limited)

Visit the Internet Music Shop at
http://www.musicsales.co.uk

Edited by Chris Charlesworth.
Cover & book designed by Michael Bell Design.
Picture research by Nikki Russell.

ISBN 0-7119-5544-1
Order No. OP47820

Exclusive Distributors:
Book Sales Limited
8/9 Frith Street,
London W1V 5TZ, UK.

Music Sales Corporation
257 Park Avenue South,
New York, NY 10010, USA.

Music Sales Pty Limited
120 Rothschild Avenue,
Rosebery, NSW 2018, Australia.

To the Music Trade only:
Music Sales Limited
8/9 Frith Street,
London W1V 5TZ, UK.

Photo credits:
Kim Tonelli/SIN: front & back cover, 16, 40, 56, 66;
All Action: 90; Piers Allardyce/SIN: 11t; Peter Anderson/SIN: 10, 33; Matt Anker/
Retna: 75, 95; Colin Bell/Retna: 6; Mark Benney/SIN: 78, 82; Jeffrey Davy/SIN: 11b;
Steve Double: 12, 14, 15t&b, 23, 28, 38, 42, 59, 69, 71, 85, 86, 88, 92; Robin Francois/
Retna: 74; Martyn Goodacre/SIN: 26, 91; Harry Goodwin: 45b; Karl Grant/Retna: 70;
Liane Hentscher/SIN: 62; Dave Hogan/All Action: 41; London Features International:
8, 9, 19, 20, 22, 24, 27, 30, 34, 37, 43, 45t, 46, 48, 51, 53, 54, 55t, 57, 58, 60, 63, 65,
80, 81, 89; Hayley Madden/SIN: 61; Lynne McAlley: 44; Peter Morris/SIN: 64;
Doug Peters/All Action: 55b; Steve Pyke/Retna: 52, 76; Rex Features: 17, 47, 50;
Ed Sirrs/Retna: 72, 84; Stills/All Action: 18, 96; Roy Tee/SIN: 4.

Printed in the United Kingdom by Scotprint, Musselburgh, Edinburgh.

A catalogue record for this book is available from the British Library.

introduction

If you believe the critics, British rock music has never been as fresh and vital as when those two supergroups, The Beatles and The Rolling Stones, did battle for pole position in the Sixties' charts. Nothing since then has come close to the excitement, the feeling that music was more than just a way of passing time.

The sound of those august penmen munching on their words could be heard in August 1995 when the simultaneous issue of singles by two groups, Blur and Oasis, made front-page headlines. And it was Blur whose 'Country House' took the honours – not by a country mile, admittedly, but it topped the pile nevertheless amid frenzied media interest.

It was the culmination of six years' work by the foursome, who started life in 1989 as a ramshackle indie act called Seymour. But those in the know could trace things even further back – another decade, in fact, to when guitarist Graham Coxon and singer Damon Albarn first hatched musical plans at school in Colchester. Damon even showed a penchant for the classics, his keyboard skills winning a heat of Young Composer of the Year.

The band first took shape at Goldsmith's College in London's New Cross where bassist Alex James was recruited. Drummer Dave Rowntree was summoned from Colchester to complete the quartet – and, since signing with Food Records and trading Seymour for a more durable name, they've never looked back.

Inevitably, the bulk of the wit and wisdom comes from frontman Damon, whose way with words is far from confined to his lyrics. Yet Blur's other three constituent parts are far from backward when it comes to expressing their views on life, the universe, and the Brit-Pop movement they and Oasis are credited with heading. And if you want to know which political leader has already been making overtures, then read on…

With the release of their fourth album, 'The Great Escape', in late 1995, Blur confirmed their position as leading lights in a music scene so newsworthy that even the Beatles have decided to make a comeback! So turn the page – and escape from reality in the company of Colchester's own Fab Four…

Mick St Michael

the early years

My dad was into psychedelia, y'know. He was one of the prime movers in the psychedelic movement – Keith Albarn, he put on Yoko Ono's first exhibition. I wanna be as important. **Damon 1990**

I always thought my parents were absolutely dead right. I was going against the grain in a weird way, by continually following my parents. It just seems to have worked for generations in my family – generations ago, we were a Quaker family, conscientious objectors, then hippies, then whatever sort of hybrid I am. **Damon 1990**

When I was at school, I never had any interest in pop music. Graham was the one who always knew about all the bands. I was just on this big, 'This-is-what's-gonna-happen' thing. It never really occurred to me that I'd be doing anything else. I guess that makes me a pretty one-dimensional person but…

I guess it's quite insane to say, from the age of 11, 'I know I'm gonna be great' but that's what I did. People thought I was a complete, big-headed twat. **Damon 1991**

This is a really lovely bit – quite Enid Blyton. We'd go for walks by the river at the back of Damon's house. One day he took me there and there was this lovely gnarled tree, and he'd got a couple of bottles of wine and tied them with strings to the roots of the tree so that they dangled in the water. He pulled one up and we sat there drinking it. That was the first time we got legless together. **Graham 1994**

I played in the school team but I was always more interested in music. I started playing the violin at the age of 12 and the two didn't really match. Music always seemed to be linked with Chelsea… and bad behaviour. Music and bad behaviour; that's what I do. **Damon 1995**

The first time I met Damon, he completely pissed me off. His music sounded like Brother Beyond. **Alex 1995**

Graham and I soon discovered that we had loads in common – including a love of booze and guitars. **Alex**

I was a part-time agit-prop-Marxist-red flag-squat-punk with a blond Mohican. **Dave 1995**

My first meeting with Damon was next to the music room practice Portakabin near the music block. But I first noticed him singing 'Please Officer Krupke' from *West Side Story* in a school assembly and I thought what a particularly extrovert chap. Completely the opposite to me, because I was very shy. Then, not long after that he had brogues that all the ska lot were wearing. I really wanted some but couldn't afford them, so I had similar things. And he came up to me and just said, 'They're crap shoes, look at these, these are the proper sort'. Then he sort of put his hair right and walked off! I thought, 'God, cheers, you know'. I don't think I'd every met anyone with such a full-on attitude. **Graham 1994**

There was a very subtle chemical change on the way from Seymour to Blur – I got into a few more drugs than I was… And that helped me a lot. It made me relax more, with bigger landscapes, bigger sounds, more lush sounds. **Damon 1990**

Seymour was the more radical, non-bite sized, unfriendly face of Blur. **Alex 1993**

We killed Seymour and changed our name. Seymour was our obtuse side. It's like if you're schizophrenic and spend six months in an institution, they cure you by leading you to the conclusion that you're better off with one side of your personality than skipping between two. I didn't think we'd do well with our obtuse side, so we made less of it. Half our personality is latent, like the sort of relationship where the physical side works best if you both dress up in leather. **Damon 1991**

When we signed to Food Records as Seymour, one of the conditions was that we changed our name. **Alex 1991**

Harmonies are perhaps the easiest thing for us – we've worked ten years on our harmonies. Graham and I used to spend every lunchtime and every first break (we were at comprehensive together – the other two went to grammar school) in the music hut – we'd play the piano and saxophone and guitar and do covers of loads of Sixties songs, folk songs, musical songs, anything. We had no choice as a lot of school songbooks of that period were Simon & Garfunkel, Lennon & McCartney – that's what we were given. **Damon 1991**

We used to hang around the music block, mainly because that was where the lads never went. They'd be off on the field playing football and beating people up. I suppose we were the school freaks in a way but we never had long hair, nothing like that. **Graham 1994**

I've completely grown up in public. I didn't know what it meant until it happened to me. I thought it was one of those things precocious people said, like Jodie Foster. But I have had to grow up in public over the last year, because I was still a teenager at the age of 26. **Damon 1995**

All the things we were into then are definitely still with us, but it

goes much deeper than that. I mean, Graham's exactly the same now as when I first met him. He looks the same, cares about the same things. **Damon 1994**

I used to go around and see him and he'd play me this weird stuff that was just endless piano, with no singing on it at all. It was just nuts. **Graham on Damon 1994**

I think I just got off on his total mad–headedness. **Graham on Damon 1991**

We were in very deep water in our early days because, basically, we didn't know what we were doing. But we did always say that we shouldn't be judged on those songs and those performances but in ten years' time. We were a fledgling group having a laugh, but we didn't have a particularly large agenda. **Damon 1994**

Blur have all got one sister and no brothers. Funny that, eh? My sister, Jessica, is younger than me. She's about to do an MA in art. She's my sister, so any things I specifically admire about her are just dwarfed by the unconditional love I feel as her brother. The relationship between older brother and sister is a weird one. I was like a cross between dad, mate, bastard and total bastard. **Damon 1993**

Hayley Coxon is my sister. She's a 30 year old nurse, a sister in fact, and she works in close conjunction with a lot of heart surgeons in the operating theatre. I admire Hayley especially because she helps save lives for a ridiculous amount of hours a week for next to no money. Purely for love. Ironically, she never noticed when I got ill the other week. **Graham 1993**

My sister lives a quiet life in Bournemouth. Like Damon's sister, she's also an artist. Having a younger sister is like having kids of your own. I remember when my mum sat down and said, 'You're having a little sister – what do you want to call her?' and I immediately said 'Deborah'. So Deborah it was. Good job I didn't say Myra. Or Adrian. That would have been silly. **Alex 1993**

My sister's called Sarah. And she's ace. Nothing to add. **Dave 1993**

I wasn't depressed at all when I was younger. I was exceptionally happy, but I was seen as being odd. I didn't want to be different, but I was. There's quite a subtle difference between wanting to be odd and actually being odd. **Damon 1995**

My grandad said 'Smile and the world will smile with you'. **Damon 1995**

I once owned up to flooding the toilets when it wasn't me. I got the slipper from the teacher for it, too. No one else would own up and we weren't allowed to go home, so I just owned up. I can't remember whether it was for anyone in particular, or whether it was a random act of chivalry – or just play stupidity. **Damon 1995**

My music teacher has recently been sent to prison for being a buttock fondler, which may explain why I never took to music lessons. **Alex 1994**

I couldn't fit in with the lads at school. I was the weirdo. Post-stroke-gay. I always got called gay. **Damon**

Damon wasn't liked (at school), and I thought he was a vain wanker. **Graham**

I was brought up in Leytonstone in a very mixed environment. From a very young age I had completely digested colour and homosexuality because my home environment was so much a part of it. Then I moved to Colchester in my teens when my dad got a job at the art college and I was actually quite shocked because I found myself in Essex, in this environment where you couldn't express yourself, you couldn't wear funny clothes and there were no black people.

   I mean, I can't believe I was born English. Why wasn't I born Spanish or West Indian? Other races seem to enjoy everything so much more. The English are mean-spirited and, yeah, I'm disappointed and ashamed and all but that's us, isn't it? That's me. I suppose our songs are just telling each other how crap we are. All my songs criticise this country. They're all about characters who are fed up and trying to get away. But they've got nowhere to go. There are mini King Canutes everywhere. **Damon 1994**

Places like Colchester celebrate the mediocre, y'know? I don't really have any fond memories of the place at all. See, places like Colchester stifle you. It's one of these places which isn't quite poverty stricken. There's a strong inclination for people to just get their lives out of the way. And that is at the centre of what we hate. Everything we do has a subtle jibe at that suburban way of thinking. **Damon 1991**

I never felt like I belonged here at all. At school I was seen as horrendously arrogant. In Colchester there's an unwritten law that you can talk about it but never achieve it. **Damon 1991**

Pop culture was never something new to me; it never served as a reference point for rebellion. I was always allowed to stay up late and stay around at parties with people smoking dope and getting pissed and taking drugs. So that never had any allure. **Damon 1995**

I saw a lot of very adult things in Turkey and was quite disturbed by it all; a Tim Drum experience really. And when I came back my parents had moved. **Damon 1995**

The girls I went out with were the ones involved with school plays – as Bohemian as you can get in an Essex comprehensive.
Damon 1995

For the first years I wasn't in love with what I was doing. I was just doing it because I'd sort of forced myself into a situation – also because I wanted to be noticed and important, but I didn't know exactly what for. And that's a very dangerous cocktail, if you're in this sort of business: it happens to a lot of the more pop-orientated people, that they want to be important. So they become pop people – but then they realise that they don't know what they're important for and they go all funny. But I found out what I'm quite good at. So I'm just normal now. **Damon 1995**

I was always a workaholic, but I just didn't have any work.
Damon 1995

Lots of people mythologise their past, and to be honest it's about time we talked about ours. The only difference is, we don't need to make anything up. I used to go to loads of parties and whenever I got there, Graham would be lying on the ground like a human doormat.
Damon 1994

I was learning to speak French during the days in 1989, Graham was putting telephones in washing-up bowls and Dave was driving a brown Ford Escort estate around Colchester and working for the council.
Alex 1995

We were young, good looking and in the best band in the world.
Damon 1994

We were a manic, completely unfocused version of what we are now.
Damon on the change from Seymour to Blur 1990

blur on blur

We'll always be friends. I like the idea of seeing each other being really old and doddery. **Alex 1994**

People are perpetually slightly confused about this band, because on one level we appear to be one thing, and on another we appear entirely different. But we're one type of band – it's just that there have been too many bands who are just one thing.
   We're not an indie band, or a rock band, or a pop band, or even a ska band. We don't really work in any genre – we're not an indie band, but we're definitely not a commercial band. We're Blur. **Damon 1991**

The concept of harmony has been there since polyphony, since Gregorian chant... I can't agree that we're a Sixties band – I think we're a very Nineties band, the only Nineties band around. If you're gonna analyse a set of individuals and their music, you've got to look further than what you see on the record. Journalists always try to look further without knowing enough. **Damon 1991**

We've always been too friendly, too clever and too good-looking for a lot of people. **Alex 1994**

I'm the George Harrison of the group. I don't do backing vocals because I prefer to look cool and smoke a fag. **Alex 1994**

We don't really go into big silent moods with each other but we're incredibly cruel to each other all the time, non stop – I mean, really cruel to the point where most people can't believe how awful we are to each other. We're just vicious, spiteful... It's mental torture, psychological warfare. **Damon 1991**

Graham has obsessions. At the moment it's American hardcore. They last from six to eight months, and it's very hard for him to see anything else. **Damon 1995**

Alex writes a song every two years and they're all about planets. **Damon 1994**

We like to think we can do anything that anyone else can do. **Damon**

I think my period of 'otherness' was just part of a transition from one mode of living to another and not really proper depression (although there are strains of it in my family), and I don't mention it because I want to jump on the misery bandwagon. If anything, it is because I loathe the idea that pop people are in a position to hand out some kind of DIY guide to depression and suicide. **Damon**

We have to put up with each other. We're four very different personalities and it's difficult if you come heavily laden with your own personality. But there's a fundamental chemistry between us and it makes things work. **Damon 1991**

The first thing Damon ever said to me was that his shoes were more expensive than mine. Eventually he went off to work in drama school in London. **Graham 1991**

We've said nothing in any of our interviews – we're probably the only band in history to do that. Dave just says nothing. Alex says nothing in an Alex way. Graham says nothing in a very negative way. I say nothing in a roundabout way.

  We do it on purpose because there is very little to say; it's all about feeling. Our generation doesn't need a spokesman. **Damon 1991**

We're miles better than spokesmen anyway – they're all wankers. We're a band without a manifesto. **Alex 1991**

We are all white, middle class, and earning a living doing what we want to do. But we are aware how privileged we are, and that's why everything comes across as being so blank. It's pathetic really, all of us constantly shoving chemicals down our throats and saying how much we love each other. But that's how we are. **Alex 1991**

I think we are very contentious. I'd like to think that by doing *Top Of The Pops* and the Radio One *Roadshow* and being ourselves, we're setting ourselves up as a ridiculous model. And this is why we're likely to become very popular. **Damon 1991**

We offer everything that all other bands together offer – we've got it all. **Damon 1993**

There's only one band in British pop who would call their album 'Modern Life Is Rubbish'. **Damon 1993**

Ours is the sort of Englishness that a war wouldn't change. It's got something to do with a latitude and a history. **Alex 1993**

We're a band who could completely and utterly change everything. The scale that we're working on is so enormous. We're trying to reach absolutely everybody. The whole world. You could never define Blur. We're just gonna be so… **Damon 1991**

Yes, we are the best group in Britain and yes, I think we probably are the best British group since The Smiths. At least in our little corner of the huge arena, if not in terms of the whole curious thing. Over a period of four years, The Smiths maintained a quality and a standard that no one else could manage, and that is our aim. Plus we have the same love-hate relationship with Britain. It annoys me when we're accused of having this

nostalgic romance with a mythical lost Britain. Where are these songs about how great the country is? Nearly every one is tempered with cynicism and aggression. **Damon 1994**

There's no mystery about why we've got so much better. We work hard. Very few bands work as hard as we do, and if you work very hard you will get better. I don't think it's about being clever. Academic cleverness doesn't really come into pop music. It's more about craftiness. A kind of instinct. **Alex 1994**

Oh dear, I think we're going to claim we've invented everything again. **Dave 1994**

We're not New Age hippies by any means, we just hate the nihilism that has existed in this country for so long. You don't get it on the continent. They've got a much healthier attitude towards being young. The English really don't like show-offs. They love it when you fail. Well, fuck them. We're not going to. **Damon 1991**

When our third album comes out our position as the quintessential English band will be assured, that is a simple statement of fact. I intend to write it in 1994. **Damon 1990**

We're far too shambolic to ever be seen as craftsmen. It's just too random what we do, that on one level we can appeal to your *Smash Hits* readers and your *Jackie* readers, and on another level we appeal to another audience and on another level. There aren't that many bands around who have that mass of randomness. **Damon 1991**

Am I a pretentious git? Probably. You've got to work out what your idea of being pretentious is. If it means you're positive about what is happening, but nothing's kind of concrete and yet you're really excited about it, for the hardened cynic – which we all are anyway – it does come across as pretentious. **Damon 1990**

People don't know how to handle me, let alone both of us! Graham saves us in a way because people can actually handle Graham. Graham's got that classic indie kind of quality about him. If we didn't have Graham in the band, we'd probably end up being Queen or something ridiculous like that. **Damon 1991**

That's why I joined Blur. I thought Damon was a bit of a wanker but he had the keys to a recording studio. **Alex 1995**

I still haven't defined where I come from. I know it's very important to people, because I've made a career out of glamorising the working class. **Damon**

Dave is learning to fly. He's almost a pilot. Who can say that out there? No-one. He's almost a pilot! **Damon 1995**

sex

I don't care who I snog, girls or boys. It's not a sexual thing at all, it's more of a header. **Damon 1991**

We're quite open about the way we feel, and that's an attractive thing. There are those two photographs of the same woman in the Desmond Morris book, 'Manwatching', one with her pupils non-dilated and one with them over-dilated. The over-dilated picture is infinitely more attractive. We're like an over-dilated pupil. Our sexuality isn't very twisted. **Damon 1991**

I have a very violent temper and I'm violent in my affections. **Damon 1991**

It's not easy for us to talk about girls. We're not very articulate on the subject. Sexual energy is too tiring for me. **Damon 1991**

It's extraordinary that 16-year olds thrust their breasts at me and ask me to sign them. But they do. **Damon 1995**

It's like, all this stuff about New Age sexuality, and how politically correct it all is. That's just a complete load of rubbish. The way people think about sex isn't remotely PC. **Damon 1994**

I used to wear women's clothing all the time when I was a kid. You know, playing in my mum's dressing-up box. It was fun. It's been quite a long time since I dressed up as a woman. Probably about a year or so. I haven't had the time to do that sort of thing recently! **Damon 1995**

Sex was probably a lot stranger when I was younger. I'm trying to rid myself of all my desires as I get older. There are certain things you have to get out of your system and I crave, erm… simplicity, these days. I don't really want to make things more complicated than they already are. **Damon 1995**

I wouldn't get a hard-on looking at a bloke but I like the idea of bisexuality. I'm more homosexual than Brett Anderson. And as far as bisexuality goes, I've had a little taste of that particular fruit, or I've been tasted, you might say. But when you get down to it, you can't beat a good pair of tits. **Damon 1994**

She makes me go faint. Especially in her early films. Nanette Newman is the ultimate housewife fantasy. **Damon 1993**

We do generally go for glamorous forty-something actresses. I find Germaine Greer terrifically sexy. She's a gardener, too, which is quite a sensual hobby. **Alex 1993**

Damon? Sexy? He's about as sexy as a stuffed fish, pal. **Graham 1994**

Girls offering sex at concerts? Something like that happens at every gig. I've had all these opportunities and I've never wanted to do it. **Damon 1991**

I think it's good for the men of Britain to have a magazine like *Loaded*, because they tend to get very confused about sex. And women like *Loaded* as well – Justine's desperate to be on the cover of *Loaded* with no top on, you know! **Damon 1995**

You can't catch anything off girls sucking your dick. **Alex 1991**

The British like sex to be a naughty thing. I think it's because we have an asexual Queen. **Damon 1994**

The Nineties are the most sexually abstract decade ever. **Damon 1994**

damon & justine

I've only ever been in love with one person and that's Justine.
Damon 1995

Justine is my best female friend, excluding my mother who is…
a mother. And I could offer about three or four male friends, but I
wouldn't want to upset any of the other ones. I'm not into defining
friendship; it's something I used to do at school. Kids need to; it's a
very brutal form of meritocracy. **Damon 1995**

Do I rip off Justine musically? Well we live together, so I suppose
there's always going to be something of that, but we like such completely
different things that it's never going to surface significantly. I mean, I love
my melodies and she loves all that noisy stuff. It's not like we're making
records that end up sounding even similar. **Damon 1995**

I don't think he's that promiscuous. He's badly behaved but I don't think
he's the slut from hell. He's a boy but he's not that sexually motivated.
He's a lot more attention motivated. I find he has one of the lowest sex
drives of any boy I've ever met. He's not that into sex. **Justine**

drugs & booze

A lot of people I know take too many drugs. It messes with their emotions, and in their quietest, darkest hours makes them very unhappy. It certainly has nothing to do with creativity. **Damon 1994**

Dragons, Apples, and Saddam Husseins! Really collectable! It'd be good to collect tabs, wouldn't it? Much better than stamps!
Alex on different acid tab types 1990

The reason we like lager is it doesn't have that dreadful rock'n'roll myth about it. It's the antithesis of 'get your rocks off'. We are astute lager louts. **Damon 1994**

Jack Daniels makes us all puke. **Graham 1994**

Would I recommend acid? Yeah, definitely, even more so than Ecstasy. It's more of a cocaine trip, whereas acid is more of a dope mentality. It's not celebrating that wonderful kind of up feeling, it's more panoramic than that, it's a more worldly drug. **Damon 1990**

The most drunk I ever got was at a private view for a college art show. I think I had two bottles of tequila and completely lost about ten hours. I woke up in a cell and, when my vision cleared, I found myself staring at a Nepalese soldier in full uniform. He didn't speak any English and he was just very alarmed that I was in there with him. When I asked the coppers what had happened, they said, 'Well, we found you at Euston station, unconscious and surrounded by a group of tramps, so we thought we'd bring you here for your own good.' I'd had all my money taken, so I had to walk home. **Damon 1995**

I mean, I've taken a bit of cocaine. Everyone I know in the music business has taken cocaine. It just didn't agree with me at all.
   People don't have to have excessive talents for it to be dangerous to them. Don't kid yourself that because you're not being like Keith Richards you're not doing yourself any harm. Oasis have gone out of their way to make themselves look working-class heroes who take lots of drugs. **Damon 1995**

I cry a lot when I'm getting very stressed. I don't cry into my beer very often, though. Occasionally, the first beer will start me off, if I'm on my own. But I'm not really a melancholy drunk. **Damon 1995**

We used to drink so much. I'd have a bottle of wine under the chair my amp was sat on, and I'd swig my way through that. **Graham 1995**

We don't drink before we go on stage, that's the only rule. **Damon 1995**

Cocaine is a stupid and dangerous drug to take. **Damon 1995**

We're just boozers, really. It's as bad as anything else, but you get spared
the claptrap. It's a good pop drug. **Alex 1994**

In the Sixties people took acid to make the world weird. Now the world
is weird, people take Prozac to make it normal. **Damon**

Until last year, I had been someone who had never in their life felt
even faintly depressed or suicidal. They were emotions that were as
foreign to me as Japanese. Then, completely out of the blue, just after
'Boys And Girls' had come out, I woke up depressed. It was like the
first day at primary school and a very bad hangover all at once…
   So I went to see a Harley Street doctor (the irony of this, I assure you,
was not lost on me) who asked me whether I had been doing any drugs.
I said a bit of cocaine, dope, quite a lot of drinking, nothing very out of
the ordinary…
   The doctor slapped my wrist, gave me some anti-depressant pills and
told me that it could take anything up to a year for me to feel completely
normal again.
   I tried the pills for a couple of days but they did nothing for me
other than make the world appear to be coming out of a transistor radio.

It was no help at all, so I stopped taking them. As our workload increased, I began to feel worse and insomnia became another little demon in my head…

To cut a few months short, I didn't go on to Prozac, take heroin or anything faintly cool or rock'n'roll. I did stop taking the small amounts of cocaine that I had done before (for people with bodies like mine, it's actually a really stupid and dangerous drug to take). I stopped drinking coffee, started playing football and going down the gym twice a week. I still drink a lot and smoke a bit of dope but generally I think I've learnt how to be a sane pop person (except at times like this when I've got jet-lag and it's five in the morning). **Damon**

rock & roll

I am part of a tradition. I am part of a music-hall-clown-entertainer tradition that's been in this country since the turn of the century. No it goes back further, to Shakespeare I guess. It's a theatrical tradition which, if you come from this country, you lean into. It's like pantomime: we're all taken to see pantos at Christmas in this country so it's in our blood. I used to love going to the pantomime. We always feel the need to entertain. That's what sets British bands apart, I think.
Damon 1995

It's always a revelation being on *Top Of The Pops*. I always feel incredibly glamorous playing around in the big time. **Damon 1991**

The best thing about being in a band is that you can allow your insanities to develop. And get paid for it. **Alex 1991**

Being in a band is like being a matador. You go out there and if you pull it off the glory is quite spectacular. But at the same time no one's going to feel sorry for you if you get gored in the stomach.
Damon 1994

There's a lot of great music being made in Britain. If punk was about getting rid of hippies, we're about getting rid of grunge. It's time kids stopped listening to American rubbish. **Damon 1995**

Being in a band is like having a mental illness, living in an institution – you became completely obsessed and ruled by your environment. And our environment is the music press, our feelings, our friends, and the audience. We work exceptionally hard. We came off tour and we've gone straight into demoing the next album immediately. **Damon 1991**

Ad Rock from The Beastie Boys is coming tonight, Alex spent a night driving round New York with Jimmy Destri of Blondie. But to be honest we don't attract celebrities. Because we don't do that many drugs, the whole aura is not people hanging out and getting really out of our faces. We don't really work like that, apart from Alex.
Damon, US tour 1995

Life's a sauna, and then you have a shower. **Alex 1991**

Of course, I'm a hedonist. What else is there to live for? The rest is just killing time. **Graham 1994**

Science hasn't been hip for a long time. It'd be good if everyone could

point to the Pole Star at a certain time every day. It'd be good to have a feeling of universal orientation. **Alex 1991**

I'm not interested in that live-young-die-fast ideal. We're anti that notion of 'authenticity'. The only truly authentic people are covers bands. **Damon 1994**

The thing you've got to understand about Blur is that there's not an ounce of rock'n'roll in us. Not any. That's why we're capable of making an album a year instead of standing around in a studio with the amps turned on waiting for the vibes. There's so much else to do. **Damon 1994**

Rock'n'roll's got a lot to do with rebellion. And the first thing you rebel against is your parents. Did you ever start to just emulate everything they thought was shit? **Alex 1990**

When my flat was burgled, I hadn't noticed. There was a keyboard missing and… some other stuff. But I couldn't bring myself to care. I mean, I never give beggars money in the street or anything so, y'know, fair's fair… **Alex 1994**

I'll tell you something funny, Alex had to be airbrushed in this picture. No, he didn't have a spot – he'd been drinking the night before and had a big double chin. They had to airbrush it out. I know what I'll do – I'll draw it back in. **Damon on the sleeve of their new album 1995**

You always remain pretty cynical if you're sensible. It's a barrier between you and the outside world. But the more things are happening to us, the more we're able to open up a bit, you know? When you do your first interviews, it's all projected ambition and they think it's all a bit big-headed. Then they start thinking, 'Oh well, they weren't such big-headed bastards after all, it's happening for them'. Then the band get a bit more of a chance to be human. If you do come across as talking rubbish, then that's fair enough. **Damon 1990**

I think there are better bands in Britain now than there have been but at the same time it's quite scary when you get reports that 'Girls And Boys' is getting played 70 times a week on KROQ. You see, I think it's important for a couple of British bands to go over there and do it completely on their own terms. My biggest hang-up with America is that it's a one-sided thing. They sell the culture wholesale, McDonalds-style to the rest of the world and they're not interested in anyone else.

   The British bands that have done well in America are the ones that have compromised themselves. Like Radiohead. That's not a criticism of them, I'm just saying that's the way they did it. But you don't last in America like that. There's not one British band who were prepared to play the game the American way and have then gone back and been accepted by an American audience a second time round. **Damon 1994**

Our audience doesn't necessarily want to get involved in the social comment and the irony of our music. But they do sense that it's trying to be brave and not just succumbing to the trauma of the Nineties. American music is the opposite – that's what it's all about. It's just translating it into an emotional thing. They're screaming in the dark, whereas we're whistling.

I want to make music for whistling in the dark. When you're a kid and you're somewhere unfamiliar, you start whistling. That's what I'm trying to do. **Damon 1995**

Pop people are defects. Pop people are funny in the head and the more pop they get, the funnier their heads become. Pop begins in bedrooms and ends up in supermarkets. **Damon**

Pop people seem to be preoccupied with not being forgotten. They are all trying to join the Immortality Club. Some try kicking down the door and shouting. 'Let me in! I'm for real, me!' Others go and give someone else's name on their application form. Some sneak in through the toilet window and a few go and kill themselves or get killed. **Damon**

Top Of The Pops is the ultimate kitsch pop experience. And the people who watch us at home, I'd like to think they're going, 'What the fuck's going on there? Beverley Craven, Bryan Adams and Blur!' **Damon 1991**

Top Of The Pops is like the London Underground. **Alex 1991**

fashion

People should be a bit more energetic. They're walking around like hippies – stooped, with greasy hair. There's no difference. **Damon 1994**

I genuinely don't know why we got roped into all those things. People say we've changed the way we look, but I was wearing a suit at Glastonbury two years ago, when the whole world had gone crusty. I'm not going to say we're ahead of our time or anything, though. Maybe people just like us. **Damon 1994**

The only image change is that I've got the money to buy more T-shirts – I wear the same clothes except more T-shirts! **Damon 1990**

I've gone Ralph Lauren mad. Well you've got to haven't yer? It's about half the price here (in Los Angeles). **Damon 1995**

All my life has been like that. One minute I'm in the East End, the next I'm transported to the outskirts of Colchester, which was practically rural. I used to come back from seeing Graham in London and then I'd go to this club called the Embassy, a real soul boy place. I'm a mixed up person. I've got this real Essex Man vibe, I can't help it. Why else do you think I still wear things like this? (solid silver bracelet). I had this real art school background, so they'd all laugh at me when I came home, because I was wearing Farah's. **Damon 1994**

We're very aware not to unleash the nasty elements – though, personally, I think I'm too camp to attract those people anyway. There's always a chance with Blur that we'll appear in a video dressed as raving fruits or schoolboys or whatever. There's no guarantee that it's gonna be just Fred Perry's and giving it what the lads want. But let's face it, we all play up to what people expect of us.

The trick is to realise that and to tell yourself that there's gonna be a cut-off point and you're gonna go on to do something else. Because the world will change anyway. That's the exciting thing for me. That's the motivation for being in a band – the fact that it's always moving. You constantly have to be on your toes. **Damon 1994**

My most treasured material possessions are these beads that I wear. My mum made them when I was about six, and in one form or another I've kept them on every day since. I take them off when we play, because once, three years ago, in Hamburg, they got pulled off. I stopped the gig, and insisted that they picked up all the beads and returned them to me before we went back on stage. They only gave me half of them back, and then last year when we played Hamburg again, a girl came up to me and gave me the rest of them back. **Damon 1995**

fame & wealth

We were being interviewed on Gary Crowley's show on GLR.
We did the interview and then we were told 'There's No Other Way'
had charted and I was grinning all over the place. It's the first midweek
position though. Our first midweek was 18, five places higher that
EMF. I just rang my mum and said, 'Y'know, it's happened at last!'
Damon 1991

It was inevitable we'd end up in the Top 10. I'd been brought up in
an off-centre way, so I understood the whole machinery. We're early
Eighties nuclear children, a product of our times, and our time is now.
Damon 1991

My mum's an artist and she recently had an opening in Sudbury and
all the people who had daughters who came to the private viewing, the
ones who knew I was going, all brought their daughters. So I got there
and first of all there was my gran, who I wasn't expecting to see and
then it was like… 'Sign this, please'… **Damon 1991**

You can tell everything about a hotel room from what sort of
Corby trouser press it's got. If its got a wall-mounted Formica 2000,
then forget it. But if it's the free-standing 3000 with electric timer,
then you're there, you've made it. **Alex 1994**

I've always known I'm incredibly special. All my life. You know?
It's not a big deal. **Damon 1991**

Some bands really think they've done well, but we've never felt like
that. **Damon 1995**

Being on *Top Of The Pops* for the first time is a massive responsibility.
It's a real honour. I mean, you're representing youth in front of this
incredible audience of 10 million people and it's your duty to… put
the knife in. That's the point when you should really start to become
incredibly great. There can be no modesty. I don't believe in modesty
when you're playing in front of 10 million people. I believe in just…
blossoming into something great, something legendary. **Damon 1991**

Everyone who's in a band thinks they're in the best band in the world.
That's only natural. But when other people start telling you you're the
best band in the world as well, you just go… *super nova confident!*
Alex 1991

I haven't worked out yet whether the secret to a happy life is getting rid of your mucky habits or doing them more. **Damon 1995**

Yes, it would be nice to win the Mercury Music Prize, but 'Parklife' has gone beyond them. We should win because the British industry ought to get behind us. They got behind Suede, but Suede haven't progressed enough and events show they couldn't handle it in the way we have. They didn't get the shit we got put through either, and neither have Oasis – I hope they don't.

But when you talk about pressure, just look at the Stone Roses or Happy Mondays... reel 'em off, they didn't survive. No, if the British music industry wants a big band again they've got to back Blur in a big way, regardless of Mercury, because we aren't going to implode. **Damon 1994**

It was quite a relief not to win the Mercury prize, because people are going to start getting fed up with us for winning everything. It's good not to achieve every time and it's important to remain some kind of underdog because there's nothing worse than a big-head. **Damon 1995**

I went to Walthamstow dogs last night, and I did a trifector, which is where you forecast the first three dogs, and I won. On a £30 bet. The odds are something like 80-1. I put it down to the fact that I wasn't drinking. The people down there couldn't believe that a pop star could also go and win so much money, so I had to buy everyone in the fucking place a drink. **Damon 1995**

Are the hordes of girls who wait, in vain usually, for a member of Take That to randomly appear at the arrivals exit at London Heathrow, mad? **Damon**

I don't feel special any more. I feel happier. **Damon 1994**

I don't feel famous at all. I've noticed it, and I suppose it's become an effort to be unfamous. It's crude, but the idea I have of myself is of someone who's getting pints of milk on the corner in the morning. **Graham 1995**

Silliness is an unavoidable state of being. When you're having to deal with something where you've become the product of a product of an even larger product, it does reduce you to buffoonery. It doesn't mean that you don't know you're doing it, though. **Damon 1991**

You're either making quality music or you're not. You're either good onstage, and you create a world that people can get it into, or you don't. The longer we hang around, the more we produce, the easier it is for people to realise that and give us some sort of respect. We're lucky to have four years' perspective. That's why the Sixties are so precious to us, that's why it's such a mesmerising time, because it has the official stamp of perspective. **Damon 1994**

We won't mention the tabloids… the most outrageous story was 'Damon was a down and out alcoholic drug addict who used to sing for his supper'. It was 'Sexy Damon of Britain's top pin-up band Blur', y'know, all the works. Better than that though, the first thing we had in the *Daily Star* was like Blur's non-stop sex and drugs lifestyle, just

two pages with photos of us… and I was coming down on the train
with my girlfriend and there was this guy in the seat opposite reading
the whole thing avidly and I was sitting there going 'Oh God'… but he
didn't twig at all. That was strange. Things like that are funny.
Damon 1991

The tabloids have always made things up. But you can always work
that to your advantage. The more they make things up, the less likely

it is people are going to believe a story that's actually true. **Damon 1994**

Fame's definitely what I wanted when I feel it's going well and I'm in control of it. I mean, I really do feel we've got the potential to be the first band in a long time to really crossover and stay noisy, y'know, mad and slightly dangerous. **Damon 1991**

I don't think any of us order people around. We might sometimes lose our temper, but it's not in our natures. **Damon 1991**

We generally pay people to order other people around now. **Dave**

I went to Capital Radio to do an interview, and David Bowie was doing the same interview, but half-an-hour later. So I arrived at the Capital building in Euston and opened the car and there were ten photographers taking my picture. That's quite an unpleasant experience. And for someone like David Bowie that must happen wherever he goes. **Damon 1991**

I wouldn't bother if I didn't think we were the best band in the universe. **Damon 1990**

Here goes my big mouth again but… the reason we're doing so well is because, at this particular moment in time, I don't think there's another band that have qualified what they're about in the world as much as we have. We've come to a point where we've really met our market full on. I know it'll change but, right now, it's all ours. When we started, I really wanted to be part of something but we're out on our own now. Untouchable. **Damon 1994**

We just went into self-destruct in '92. There was this general sense that we were redundant and, quite naturally, we couldn't handle it… that was totally rock bottom. All we had left was ourselves in a studio in Fulham. But, when you've got absolutely nothing to lose, you sometimes come out with your best material. **Damon 1994**

Our pride was very bashed and we decided that it wasn't good for us mentally to be in that anxious, paranoid state. Part of it was like driving a car and wanting to crash it so the responsibility of driving it isn't there anymore.
   The fact that Suede were doing so well really helped. I remember we came back from America and suddenly Suede were everywhere and we were crap. That was weird. I went down the Underworld and no-one wanted to talk to me. I was yesterday's guitar man. And it mattered! We don't like people stealing our thunder! We tend to think that we've earned a right to a certain amount. It's that simple. And we're very affronted when we're ignored. **Graham 1994**

I'm pretty brutal. I don't fear aggression. Obviously, I don't
wanna get my 'ead kicked in, but I don't mind arguing. Y'know, some
people, it affects their whole being when they're in confrontation,
but I'm not like that. I enjoy a good barney. **Damon 1994**

Stars are back, that's for sure. There hasn't been a star drummer or
a star bass player or even a star guitarist for years but I think that's all
coming back. **Alex 1991**

If you believe in something so much then you've got to believe in
having control over it. You can't trust anyone. To let any part of it
out of your hands, you've got to assess whether the other person's
motivation to help and understand you is in line with their own
self-interest…
    What's the problem with being cynical? It's not as if you're losing
your soul because you're a cynic. British music has had this problem
for a while – the idea that you lose your soul if you suddenly become
too in control or knowing about things. That's total bollocks, really.
Damon 1991

The only thing you can do about it is convince the people at the top
that you are the most marketable image, not The Doors. Having said
that, I don't mean you should go about it thinking you're gonna have
a marketable image, you just have to get to these people and convince
them that what you are is marketable.
    I don't feel that's impossible. I mean, Jim Morrison will be the
image this year but I don't think that really matters to us because it's so
obvious what it's all about. I mean, I'm sure a Doors song will be used
in a Levi's ad and will go to Number One and everything. But that's
just using a pop icon to serve another, more powerful icon, the icon
of possession.
    When we've convinced the powers that be that we are as marketable
an image as The Doors, it'll be the other way round, the product will
be serving us. That's the only way it can work these days, because all
the great taboos like taking your trousers off or being sick on stage and
all that kind of 'Fuck the system' have all gone, they've all been done,
so subversion's getting darker and more sinister. There's certainly
something subversive about us but it's probably a bit more kind of…
psychiatric as opposed to obvious. **Damon 1991**

Prior to 'Parklife' we lived in our own little world. And now the world
lives in our… little world. Basically, there's no longer any need for us
to feel like a gang. **Damon 1995**

We all need each other's support or criticism, though. I wouldn't be
comfortable doing a lot unless it could be checked out by other people,
I trust Stephen (Street) quite a bit. **Graham 1995**

I think the single 'Girls And Boys' was the first big crossover record
for a British band since, erm, whenever. It kind of started with that.
You know you're a household name when things become unpleasant
with the tabloid newspapers, but you should be able to get around the
most stupid things by approaching them on a stupid level. It's pop
music. It's not supposed to be taken too seriously, is it? **Damon 1995**

The biggest myth about fame is that it makes you feel somehow
enlightened. It actually makes you feel disabled. It's the equivalent of
having no arm and walking down the street. Everyone looks at you.
Fame is just a condition. **Damon 1995**

It's only recently that I think we've really cared whether the people in America really care about us or not. We spent so much time arguing with our record company over there because they didn't seem to get what we were doing at all. We've changed to Virgin there now and the people we're dealing with seem all right. **Dave 1995**

Yeah, it all looks like chaos, but we make chaos look easy. It looks like it's going to fall apart any minute, but it doesn't. And that actually takes a lot of work. I don't think we've ever played a gig in Britain where we've completely fucked up. We're always entertaining in some way. **Damon 1995**

I realise that when you get in the Top 10, you do say things and you do make mistakes, but then you have to make a decision about what you want to do. We got especially pissed off with all the tabloid and teen press we received, but we do know what we are doing here and we're in a position to say we're not going to do it any more. **Damon 1991**

Ultimately, I think we write better songs than everybody else, so of course we're going to carry on being around. **Damon 1993**

I think that people like to keep their distance from us. It's all quite voyeuristic at the moment. I think they find us sort of stand-offish. But they're definitely interested. **Damon 1991**

You see you've got to be very careful preaching to people that young. I was quoted recently as saying that Morrissey and Robert Smith had a really bad influence on people, that their lyrics were a 'cerebral minefield'. If you take these people literally – and certainly a lot of people did – and it happens to be a critical time in your life, you can get very seriously screwed up with that negative vibe going round in your head. **Damon 1991**

A year ago our view of what it would be like to be famous was very romantic. That can't help you at all when you've got to deal with the sheer… day-to-dayness of it all. To have your life filmed as you live. **Damon 1991**

You become totally aware of your every action. It's a very weird thing not to be able to walk to the shops without thinking of yourself as the guitarist in Blur walking to the shops. **Graham 1991**

We haven't had screaming girls at gigs for quite a while, but we might again now. I can handle intellectual appreciation and I can handle screaming girls. I know that our looks have got up people's noses in the past. That's bound to happen. And if this album does what it's set out to we'll get up even more noses, because we'll be really in people's faces. **Damon 1994**

The last year has taught me that you really can get caught up in the idea that more is better, and it just isn't. There are zillions of records sold that just won't be remembered even five years later. **Damon 1995**

'The Great Escape' was made at such a transitional period in our lives, and we've got over that hurdle now. It was stupid for a while. Winning four Brits was an odd experience. It caught everyone by surprise. **Damon 1995**

I enjoyed presenting *Top Of The Pops*, but I was quite nervous at the time. I think I said too many lines, there were ten second periods in which to do your bit and the seasoned presenter just says 'And now, on *Top Of The Pops*', you know. But I enjoyed it. It was good… I'd like to present *Grandstand* and *Desert Island Discs*. **Damon 1995**

I don't want to come across as satisfied because I'm not. It's just that the success of 'Parklife' has given me a lot more confidence. **Damon 1994**

While we were in the States, we discovered that all the money we'd made from 'Leisure' – which wasn't millions, but quite a reasonable amount – had 'disappeared'. We'd worked as hard as people like Ride or The Charlatans, but we hadn't seen anything. We literally had no money; we couldn't even pay our rent, and it got to the stage where it was touch and go whether or not we'd go bankrupt. **Damon 1992**

I don't feel famous at all. I've noticed it, and I suppose it's become an effort to be unfamous. **Graham 1995**

There was a time when any pop star who even admitted to enjoying books was dismissed as a middle-class twat. They've virtually given up on calling me a middle-class twat now because I've actually admitted, 'Yes, I am a middle-class twat' about a million times, so they've given up now! **Damon 1995**

They love me in the tabloids because I'm sort of 'Woargh, lager, lager, hur, hur'. The tabloid side is incredibly easy – you just get drunk occasionally and go to the football. That's all you have to do. Oh, and say 'birds' and 'tits' – and you're laughing.

  But then *The Guardian* loves me as well, and Radio 4. But I don't mind. I like to be in a bit of everything. I'm one of those people who's never too sure of who they really are, so one has to try to be everything all at once. I'm terribly insecure! It's as though I have to feel liked. But courting the media is not something I'm conscious of doing. **Damon 1995**

fans

There's always a Jimmy from *Quadrophenia* lookalike at our gigs. Last night's was brilliant. Looked like him, talked like him, wore exactly the same clothes. Never seen the film! **Dave 1994**

Japanese audiences dye their hair blond, dress in Adidas zip-ups and Fred Perry tops – and then they put ties on as well. It's very strange... **Graham 1994**

We understood what the Nineties were about when we started. We had the zeitgeist already in place. I suppose that's inevitable, because we are a Nineties band. We're Nineties eaters. Last year, we built up a considerable fan base on what on the surface looked like a king of mod revivalism, but it's not that. Our audience have the same feelings about the Nineties as we do. **Damon 1994**

I've got people camping outside my place in Kensington. In sleeping bags. It's not that irritating, except we haven't got any curtains in the front room, so we can't walk round in the nude. **Damon 1994**

This girl rang us up in Leicester and wanted to speak to me. When I got on the phone there was this silence, so I said, 'Hello, who's there?' and there was this incredible scream. It was like, 'Oh my God! Oh my God! I think I'm gonna cry! Dad! Dad! I've got in contact with him!' I managed to calm her down and said I'd put her on the guest-list for the next night but she arrived in Sheffield at eight the next morning and she had everything that's ever been written about us in this big book. She was taking pictures of us and everything, she even took pictures of the stage getting set up. It was weird. She gave me this gold ring and when I gave it back to her she broke down and said she'd never touch it again. She came into the dressing-room and burst into tears and ran off. She was an ex-Brosette. Matt Goss had told her to fuck off out of it once and I think she was a little overwhelmed that we didn't do the same thing. **Damon 1990**

Oh yeah, we've got all these Japanese girls that follow us around. They're completely mad. They're so polite and they've got these incredibly expensive video-cameras. They love waving too, when you get on the bus they all wave. It's like their idea of sex is waving and bowing. **Damon 1990**

Oh the guys, they do have this one obsession. I have to draw the logo on so many boys' bums, on their jeans pockets. It's outrageous. **Graham 1990**

It's weird because with guys it's not a love thing, it's more of a 'Let's be mates, let's get onstage and, woargh, nice one!' sort of thing. It's funny, I really love that. If that's as far as I ever get in communicating with people, that's great. I just like the idea of everyone cuddling each other. **Damon 1990**

People have been throwing betting slips onstage. And, since the album came out, we've heard that some owner had named his dog Parklife! **Damon 1994**

heroes & influences

It was a privilege to work with Phil Daniels on our album because in the afterglow of Mike Leigh, I sort of feel that what Phil does best has been hijacked. And what Phil does to a large extent is sort of our bag really. He's been a bit left out, with Tim Roth and Gary Oldman becoming real names in Hollywood, and the press loving anything American-related. Phil has a brilliantly unnerving quality about him, though. I really feel at ease in his company. **Damon 1993**

The Who was the main influence in the early days. That and Mike Leigh films. Graham had a Who video and a Mike Leigh video and that's all we watched. That's all you need… (That and biscuits and tea! – Graham) **Damon 1994**

We're influenced by adverts and Sunday magazines and slogans around us. Things people say in films and certain moments of programmes like *Come Dancing*. Just little moments, strange stances and gestures – the madness of human behaviour – are what gets us through the night. **Damon 1991**

Not liking Guns N'Roses is like not liking Madonna or like trying to stop the world going round. Whatever we say… it won't make any difference. **Alex 1995**

We first met at 13, but 14 was the 'proper' time. It was at school near a Portakabin. There was a music Portakabin. I wanted to be Keith Moon and Damon wanted to be Roger Daltrey… (No, I wanted to be Keith Moon, too! – Damon) **Graham 1994**

When I was 16, the Smiths were the best band in the world. We all wanted to dress like Morrissey, give up meat like Morrissey, and some of us went the whole hog and became Morrissey. The most important thing if you were Morrissey was to be miserable, so if you wanted to be Morrissey, you were miserable, too.

Yes, I have a very cynical perspective but pop people have pop emotions and they are not be trusted. If Morrissey and happy Kurt gave you a run for your money, they are nothing on Courtney Love. She makes them seem bland.

I've always thought her and Pamela Anderson should merge into one being: Pamela Love, the Tabloid Medusa. **Damon**

Justine has been playing a lot of Ella Fitzgerald records around the house recently, and getting me into her as a result. There's nothing to beat the sound of Ella Fitzgerald singing Kurt Weill or Cole Porter. **Damon 1993**

When we were recording 'Modern Life'... 'Generation X' by Douglas Coupland was a really big influence on me, but for the new one it was 'London Fields' by Martin Amis. I couldn't get over how much I loved that book, it had so many different levels. London's like something you fall in love with. It's when it gives you the clap that you really find out how much it means to you. **Damon 1994**

I don't understand how Tony Benn comes to be known as this barmy left-wing radical when there's nothing the remotest bit sinister about him, just this very straightforward, generous man. Tony Benn is an eminently trustworthy proponent of straightforward values. He renounced his peerage, and was instrumental in the Labour government in the year following the massive implementation of a welfare state programme. And, at the moment, when there are so few people left in politics who originally helped instigate the welfare state, and so may trying to undermine it, Tony Benn is symbolic of the values that post-war Britain stood for. **Damon 1993**

There was this brilliant programme on Tony Benn a while ago on Radio 4. It might have been *The Benn Diaries*, actually, where he was being investigated by MI5. He already knew his phone was being tapped and he would look out the window, see a black car screeching to a halt and these figures would jump out and run off with his rubbish, in order to try and nail him with incriminating evidence. A hero, basically. **Alex 1993**

Herman Hesse was the first writer who actually had any effect on me. All his books seemed totally at odds with the 20th Century, he never had any pretence of trying to be a futurist, there was never an agenda. All his books were good, but I suppose the key ones were 'Steppenwolf' and 'Siddhartha'. He was always trying to define a spirituality but at the same time he stayed clear of any sex or dogma. He was just there. One of the first urban pagans. **Damon 1993**

Lobsang Ranpas was a Tibetan monk who had to escape when the Chinese invaded and he wrote a book called 'The Third Eye'. It's a trashy little novel which isn't really of any literary worth but I just became quite obsessed with it. I love the idea of Tibet and I've always wanted to go there. I don't really know why, it's just one of those things. Some people like dinosaurs, some like motorbikes. I like Tibet. I suppose it's to do with having hippy parents as well, my mum went there recently and she absolutely loved it. But there's a good deal of duality about it, it is the spiritual centre of the entire earth. One day I'll go. **Damon 1993**

Lindsay Kemp's a dancer but it's very hard to define exactly what he does. He's a fat, bald, homosexual Englishman who worked with

David Bowie for a while and only comes over here once a year. I was always told about him as a child by my parents, and I finally got to see him abut two years ago. Though I don't like dance really, he just had a spirit about him. The show I saw was quite improvised, he just dances. It didn't really have any form but he's got a freedom in the way he moves. I really love the way that he's past 60 but still puts on his tights and dancing shoes and prances around on stage. I think that's wonderful and that's what I aspire to do when I'm 60. Only I'll wear DMs. **Damon 1993**

There's one film by Mike Leigh called *Meantime* which I watched every day at lunchtime because Graham lived next door to school and we'd watch it again and again. We know every single word. Graham was always Colin, who was Daniels' brother, and I was Phil Daniels. And of course there was *Quadrophenia*. What a film! Daniels just represents everything I would like to be if I wasn't who I was. I love the way he's avoided going to America, like I heard Gary Oldman on television the other day and he's adopted this LA accent, which seems so desperate. Phil Daniels has retained his identity throughout his career, and of all that new wave of British actors he's the one I most admire. I went to drama school but I realised after a year that I was the worst actor on earth, so I appreciate how difficult it's been for Daniels to remain Daniels throughout his career. **Damon 1993**

I used to just cook pasta with tinned tomatoes and sweetcorn until I watched Keith Floyd in Majorca and it literally changed my life. Every other cook I'd watched made it look like a real chore and a science to cook, but Floyd was there taking the piss and getting pissed and he made it look like fun. I haven't looked back since then. I love cooking now, it's my main hobby. So he was very important to me. One of my favourite people. **Damon 1993**

I am genuinely inspired by my mum. I love and respect my mum and I think she's great. She always makes me laugh and I trust her totally. Both my parents are artists and I grew up in quite a liberal home; I was allowed to do what I wanted, but all based on a strong moral foundation. I think it's really important that parents allow you to do what you like when you're young because you're more likely to get it all out of your system. I do love my mum. **Damon 1993**

Francoise Hardy's a French chanteuse, and probably the most popular French singer. She wrote with this other bloke but I've forgotten his name – should've done my homework.

Hardy was a singer-songwriter who wrote about love, very beautifully arranged songs. I got into her after I couldn't handle listening to noise any more and I wanted to listen to something beautiful. I got very into the kind of emotional and tragic music that started in the early '60s. I always buy her albums whenever I see them. What I like is that it's an unlimited experience because I can't speak French, so I get more out of the sounds and arrangements than I do from the lyrics.

She was just a classic-looking French woman who sang about heartache. Some of it is jolly but the depressing stuff is the best, although it's still an elation because the songs are so amazing – a tidal wave of emotion. She's sadly missed – she's not dead, just out of action. Last thing I heard she was doing horoscopes.

She's a goddess and a genius. **Graham 1994**

Rod Stewart's 'First Cut Is The Deepest' – I played it over and over again, I had to. I played it beyond the point of nausea and it was still great. **Damon 1990**

The Specials were a high point of British pop culture and it's something I really aspire to create again. **Damon 1994**

Look at Ken Livingstone – I'd like to see him as the William Tell of England! **Damon 1995**

It was one of the biggest thrills of my life when Phil Daniels performed with us at Shepherd's Bush. I didn't know what he was going to do. In the rehearsal, he changed the words to 'Damon's got a brewer's droop' so God knows what he was gonna say. **Damon 1994**

We're very dissatisfied with anything that isn't slightly… twisted. I like people like John Lennon who are stars in a totally anti-star way. **Graham 1991**

It's not quite as bad as 'I hope he dies from Aids' (Noel Gallagher's attack on Damon), but it's the same sort of idiotic thing that'll always turn up the press. It was misinterpreted. I wasn't really having a go at him, I was just saying it was stupid to take heroin. He wasn't looking very healthy at the time, and I think maybe sometimes when people say something about you in the press, it can really bring it home to you. But I'm not trying to justify it at all. I was out of order to say what I said… and I'm sorry. **Damon on his public war of words with Brett Anderson from Suede 1995**

Shoegazing was a term invented by Andy Ross to describe all the bands that we weren't. They were shoegazers. That's precisely what we weren't. Then we went to France and there were all these questions about shoegazers. **Alex 1994**

The only tradition I've ever felt comfortable with is the British art-school group tradition… and when I think about some of the groups from that background I'd probably rather be like Talking Heads. **Damon 1994**

The Kinks had an enormous effect on me the first time I heard them, and the first Kinks record I was really aware of was 'Lola'. In fact I heard 'Lola' for the first time when I was 13 – in Germany, of all places!

We were on a school exchange in the summer holidays, in a small village called Erder, in the hills behind Wetzlar. I remember it very clearly. I was watching TV when the Kinks came on – so I realised that the Kinks were my band while I was in the hills of Germany.

I think I got on well with him – as well as anyone can get on with Ray Davies, that is. We did an interview together once, after we'd already met five or six times, and the first question from the interviewer was 'Do you like each other now you've met several times?' and Ray just adjusted his hat and said, 'I very rarely use the word like.' So, you know, there's a man who lives in his own hat. He's part of that English tradition of eccentricity. **Damon 1995**

Monie Love represents a lot of very significant things for me. She reminds me of a couple of West Indian girls in my neighbourhood who I used to go out with. I only like some of her records, but I adore the way she carries herself. Her interviews are always really funny. It was also really cool the way she just upped and left for America, without really knowing anyone, and became adopted by De La Soul, the Jungle Brothers, Queen Latifah and all their mates. This London street urchin, you know? **Damon 1993**

Well, when it comes to fellas, I like a bit of a thinker, and they don't come much better than Isaac Newton. All knowledge that we have in science is based on Einstein's Theory of Relativity, Newton's Law of Gravity and Quantum Theory, and they all contradict each other. But Newton was the bloke who realised that everything was in motion, I mean, fucking hell! How do you suddenly realise that? I dunno, I suppose anyone could have realised it, but to work out the theory that verifies it is stunning. **Alex 1993**

Continuing with my theme of people who bring knowledge to bear on the lives of the masses, I'd like to nominate Carol Vorderman as one of my favourite girls. She makes mathematics a joy to watch, while taking so much stick from that wooden bloke. **Alex 1993**

Even though I'm a Chelsea fan, there's no getting around Ryan Giggs' genius. For the fact that you can walk into any pub across the land and guarantee that there'll be a conversation about him taking place. The last time that happened was with George Best. **Damon 1993**

Brian Johnston used to make my Sundays. He was the last of the old school of sports commentators. I used to watch the cricket on the telly with the sound down, just so that I could have the radio on with his beautiful voice. **Dave 1993**

I've always had a bit of a Malcolm McDowell fixation. **Damon 1995**

politics & patriotism

Britain's not necessarily a great place, but what it does possess is a peculiar perspective on the world. We're a minute island in Europe that once ruled virtually half the world and that has The Beatles and the Queen – all these relics. And so culturally we still count, because occasionally something from this country gets through the net and gets embraced by McDonalds and Sony and Coca Cola and then becomes all-encompassing. **Damon 1995**

They asked me to provide the voice for a very dull man with a grating, nasal voice – presumably because the Prime Minister wasn't available. **Ken Livingstone 1995**

I'm supposed to be spokesperson for an entire generation! Did you know the Labour Party asked me to the Houses of Parliament to see what I think. Tony Blair got me in there.
  I told them 'You're only gonna win if you can convince the kids that life will be better if they register to vote.' So many dropped off the register because of the poll tax. So there's a whole sea of non-voters out there. **Damon 1995**

The Englishness that we celebrate isn't real Englishness. It's an imaginary Englishness. It's kind of halfway between a piss-take and serious disillusion. **Graham 1991**

The National Front/British Nationalist Party are my enemies simply because they're just vile. They have no real manifesto, it's built completely on hate and distrust. I just can't believe it when I hear people prattling on about them in pubs and saying things like 'that f— ing nigger', it's disgusting. I go to football quite a lot to see Chelsea and some of the boys in the Shed are beyond belief. They really are villains, big villains. I didn't have that much contact with Nazis when I was growing up, because I grew up in the East End and most of my friends were black – my first girlfriend was a West Indian. But then I moved to Colchester and I was really aware of it there. There was one black person at school and you can imagine the sort of reception he got. Essex is a very right wing place which is why I hate going back there. **Damon 1993**

We sing about this country and how we feel about it. We tell stories. **Damon 1994**

Coca Cola is one of my arch rivals because it embodies all the dreadful things about the present day. It's just sugar, basically, and sugar is a drug that is given to kids when they're really young which becomes part of your personality and you crave that adrenalin and it's symptomatic of violence. And the way the corporation spearheaded the global marketing campaigns like making Diet Coke embody the Eighties and that body beautiful obsession. It's the cloning aspect of it as well. And the adverts were attractive West Coast white girls. But now they've moved into Coca Cola clear, that's the most scary because that is just sugar. They're the non-emotional despot of our society. **Damon 1993**

I support Viva!'s CRATE (Campaign To Resist Animal Transport to Europe) campaign, because live exports should be banned. Without compassion, there is little hope for any of us – we've got to change the world for the better.

  I hope that as individuals and as a band, we can make some contribution to raising people's general awareness of animal welfare in the years to come...

  Anyone who uses violence must realise it's not a reasonable way you achieve your aims. After all, it's the violence towards animals that we're trying to stop, so it's hypocritical. Violence isn't the way to achieve anything. **Damon 1995**

The Shopping Channel's not here yet, but it's coming and I think it's fairly well known that I'm not that keen on consumerism. It's an enormous industry – people literally don't have to leave their homes because they've everything at their fingertips. It's like *The Stepford Wives* or something! It's the height of American consumerism, where you don't have to leave your living room to go shopping, which I love. But it's coming to England. Beware! **Damon 1993**

I can't believe Rupert Murdoch's just a businessman, there's no such thing. He just peddles shit, he has no quality control at all. He's no doubt one of the people around whom the whole conspiracy theory is built. I'd go on about the Masons as well but, well, you can't be too careful... **Damon 1993**

I know they couldn't help it, but it was the last straw for me. It just showed how crap we are, how crap we've become. And it signalled that we've accepted that we're about to be vacuumed up by the good ol' US of A on every front. Football at home, week to week, is still brilliant, but that was a very sad day on the whole. It was a sad, sad day. **Damon on England's defeat by the USA 1993**

The people who buy our records couldn't care less about what America thinks or does. Why does everybody else have to worry so much? **Damon 1994**

From my background, much as I despise radical Christians or radical Moslems, they believe in what they believe. It comes across as immense arrogance, but to them it's as much a belief as falling in love with someone. **Damon 1990**

What do we stand for? So we don't lie down all the time! **Damon 1991**

I feel an all-consuming feeling that we're laying our world to waste and there's little I can do about it except say there's nothing I can do, and eat Indian curry. **Damon 1991**

The Nineties are the remnants of whatever going down the plughole. The Nineties are the end of a millenium, they're not just the end of a decade or a century. It's a profound menopausal experience mankind is going through. **Damon 1993**

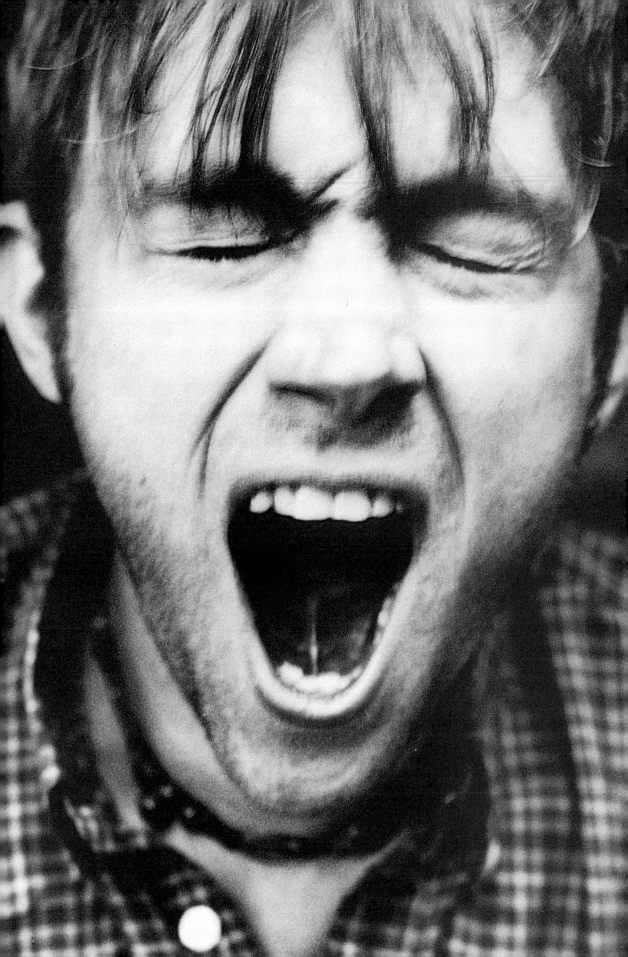

other groups

I'm not interested in other bands, I don't enjoy going to see them.
I do like music, but it's not important to us as Blur. It's not relevant.
Of course there have been great songwriters, but we're just trying
to start it all over again. **Damon 1990**

We'll blow REM off stage. Or, to be diplomatic, we'll give
them a run for their money. When we agreed to do it, 'Parklife'
hadn't even gone platinum. Now it's sold a million, which is as
much as any of their albums have in the UK. It'll be an interesting day,
because you rarely get two bands of that size playing together.
Damon at Milton Keynes 1995

Playing with REM is like playing with U2 – you never know
what they're going to do. **Alex 1995**

Take someone like Daniel Day-Lewis. I hate cunts like that,
they're the bane of my life, these people who think they're tortured.
They always need someone else to make them good. Where would
Morrissey be without Johnny Marr? He's a lager-eater! **Damon 1994**

Look, I don't wanna talk about the Suede thing because I've
exorcised all of my little hang-ups. I imposed them on myself in the
first place and they were probably unnecessary but it helped them in
the first place and it sure helped us. But now I think it's quits. I mean,
we're pretty similar really. I object to some of the things I've seen that
I've said. Y'know, I'm very negative and it's unnecessary sometimes.
Damon 1992

Mr Butler was Blur's guitar roadie for two years… he spent hours
crying on my doorstep for us to take him on tour. **Graham on the
former Suede guitarist 1994**

This is the first time we've spoken about this (Suede v Blur),
because we didn't want to come across as vindictive. We wanted to
wait until we were at the top to reveal these stories. If we'd said all
this two years ago, no-one would have believed us. I knew that my
moment for vengeance would come. Public vengeance and personal
vengeance. I wanted to prove to myself that I could dethrone Brett
and his group of cretins. We'll see who's at the top of the charts in
two or three years. **Damon 1992**

For the record, I think Suede are a very important band but they've

got to go through similar things to what we've been through. It hurts
when you see yourself ignored and other people taken notice of.
Damon 1994

I can appreciate that we generate a similar feel to Primal Scream but
I just don't share the same vision. We did all our drugs before we were
in this band. **Damon 1994**

To be honest, I'm more worried about Morrissey's records which
I think are… if not appalling, certainly not great. Y'know, he's lost
all enthusiasm. That renders all the rest of it impotent, really, that
the music isn't up to scratch. He wouldn't have to bother with the
outrage if it was. **Damon 1994**

Although we're totally unlike him, there is a similarity between us
and Jonathan Ross. He's somebody who's slowly becoming part of
the everyday consciousness because he's jarring – a lot of people either
absolutely love him or absolutely hate him so it's inevitable, if he
comes across something very different but also the same, something
like us, that he would react against it. I wouldn't really want him
to like us to be honest. **Damon 1991**

Mick Jagger – he was brilliant. There's stories about him at parties,
talking to, like, groupies in one room and then lawyers and accountants
in another. **Damon 1991**

The Pixies are the last great American band. They piss on Nirvana.
Alex 1995

I think there are three Bob Dylans, playing simultaneously, around the
world. I believe this because he always looks the same – dark glasses,
scarf, big hat – and he sings every single song with the same note. One
of the three is the real one. We played with him at a festival in Milan
and I just knew it wasn't Bob Dylan… **Damon 1995**

Actually, what I'd like to see is Morrissey sing a Cole Porter song,
because I was listening to his new album and I discovered that 'I Am
Hated For Loving' has a seventh chord, which means that Morrissey
has to sing a passing blues note over it, and it totally reveals that he
can only sing about four notes. So that's my big challenge to Morrissey:
sing a Cole Porter song! Moz's new album sounds out of tune and a
little bit clumsy. **Damon 1993**

I don't think you'd have Suede without Blur. Well, I know you
wouldn't. Listen their first interviews applauded the idea of writing
pop songs, being massive, being pop stars and being very English.
They were things we were laughed at for saying. **Damon 1993**

I met Shaun Ryder last night and his new group Black Grape is similar (to Blur). Shaun is definitely a wise fool: he's a bright bloke. Having Bez in there just as a dancer is brilliant theatre – and Shaun understands that. **Damon 1995**

Suede – borrowed money, borrowed talent, borrowed quotes, borrowed time… at a good rate of interest. **Alex 1993**

I actually see a lot of similarities between us and The Smiths, but Morrissey, at the end of The Smiths, going on national television and saying that they had been the last group of any importance, showed that the conceit of the man has made him oblivious to the plight of… well never mind his own audience, the plight of us all. **Damon 1991**

It had got to the stage where every time I got drunk I got very nasty about Suede. I just couldn't see the wood for the trees because of Justine. They felt slighted and they wanted revenge, I can understand they hated us with a passion. And I knew from the things they said that they were going to be big. I was just in a very bad way. **Damon 1994**

We really annoy our peers quite immensely. Which is amusing. The Manic Street Preachers feel compelled to indulge in onstage outbursts about us. **Damon 1994**

Perhaps I'm biased, but Justine and Elastica have worked harder than any other British band in America. They've done three six-week tours this year, and that's a hell of a lot. With Lollapalooza, it's four. And it seems to me like that's the only way you can do it. We're just not one of those bands that can do that without just… losing it. **Damon 1995**

Pulp are one of my favourites. We've done a lot of growing up together. What I love about them is that they're bright. **Damon 1995**

We don't have any plans to work with Brian Eno. Look what he's done to David Bowie. Or has David Bowie done it to him? But the main thing, regardless of good intentions, is that if you aren't writing good tunes, it's over. Forget it! **Damon 1995**

Lisa Stansfield is really British. She's our Whitney Houston. **Alex 1995**

blur v. oasis

The feud between the bands came to a head in August 1995 when the two released singles, 'Country House' and 'Roll With It', in direct competition. Blur won the race to Number One by a short head.

Blur had better enjoy their celebrations now because it will be a different story on Sunday. **Spokesperson for Oasis**

More than competition with Oasis, though, it's competition with ourselves. We just want to do better than we've done before. We've never had a Number One single. We want one. **Damon**

We thought this would be an easier way to settle our differences than having a punch-up – and hopefully less blood will be shed. May the best band win. Whatever happens we won't be talking to each other next week. **Damon 1995**

It's important that Oasis are rude about everybody and that they get drunk. That's what people like you want, and you encourage them. Fair enough. It's nice, isn't it? But it's nothing to do with me. They came to see us in Manchester and they were very pleasant boys. Very nice. I'd like to see that as a quote. Oasis are very nice boys. **Damon**

I would have been disappointed if Oasis had got to Number One instead of us. But I think they're a really good band and this rivalry is just getting silly now. At the Brit Awards – and I know we won a lot and that annoyed them – when I said, 'This should be shared with Oasis', I thought that was the fair thing to say. After that, they were fine in person but in public they were still equally aggressive about the whole thing. When they got to Number One with 'Some Might Say', I went down to their party to have a drink and congratulate them. You know, they'd got something I'd been dreaming about all my life.

So I went down there and said, 'Well done, Liam'. But then he puts his face right up to mine – so that our noses are touching – sticks out one finger and goes, 'We're Number One, mate, Number One!' I don't know why I bothered going, as I wasn't even vaguely happy for him. I'm quite a competitive person and he just humiliated me. I just thought, 'I really don't need this'. **Damon**

Suede don't really fit in. It's Oasis or us. **Damon**

Both the singles are very strong and I really don't know what's going to go in higher. It's too exciting to bet on. The idea that the rivalry is like The Beatles and the Stones is right. Oasis and Blur are both big British bands, they're the only ones who could do this. 'Clash Of The Titans' is the thing that springs to mind. ***Top Of The Pops* producer Ric Blaxill**

Suddenly there would appear to be some kind of feud between the bands. But the 14 August date hadn't even occurred to us until today. It won't be a problem to play both videos if they are of good quality. There's no pecking order between them as far as we're concerned. We don't look backwards at previous chart placings, we look forwards. ***Chart Show* producer Phil Davey**

It's brilliant that there are two relatively new English acts who can do this. The thing I like best about it is that Madonna is releasing a single on the same day and nobody gives a shit because of Blur and Oasis. But it's unfair to make a prediction. I work with both bands. **MCP Promoters' Tim Parsons**

Sometimes there's nothing better than a head-on clash. It reminds all the minions at record companies that they have a job to do. It's totally healthy. It comes at a time when music is a little more exciting. I saw Blur and Oasis at the Brits. It was the first time I'd been in Britain and *compos mentis* for about five years. I'm not sure who'll go into the chart higher. But I'm more familiar with Blur. **Rolling Stones' ex-manager Andrew Oldham**

I think it's great. It's conflict. Conflict, conflict, conflict. I have split loyalties because I'm a great friend of Blur's producer Stephen Street but I'm from Manchester and I'm an Oasis fan. If I had to choose

between them, I'd go for Oasis by a long way. But I wouldn't bet
a penny of my money until I'd heard both songs. **Factory Records
boss Tony Wilson**

The record has gone straight onto the A-list at Radio 1 and will get
between 25 and 31 plays so I'm over the moon. Our job is to make
sure all the producers have the record well in advance and that they
want to play it. We started off with *The Evening Session* on 13 July
and Oasis were on 17 July. Blur wanted *The Evening Session* to be first.
So many people wanted the single and people were even threatening to
play it off the pre-release tape. As soon as we had the finished product
the radio had it. It came in on the Thursday and it was played on the
Thursday. It was like opening the floodgates. I would be very surprised
if the Blur single doesn't get to Number One.' **Parlophone radio
plugger Phil Gibbs**

I don't regard it as a competition between bands. It's a competition
between rock'n'roll and bland. It's about Oasis and Blur versus Bon
Jovi, Celine Dion and Tina Arena. Radio 1 are playing them both,
GLR and Virgin are playing them both, Atlantic 252 plays Oasis and
Capital are starting to play Oasis, too. It's like when REM started, nine
of the stations wanted to know about them in 1983 but then it built.
I think the Blur/Oasis thing will carry on into 1996. The important
thing is that they do well in America and Australia and Japan and all
over the world. **Independent radio plugger Dylan White**

I'm delighted that they're having this face-off. They're living
The Beatles and the Stones legend which is quite exciting. Both bands
have come up with singles that are fairly typical, but maybe the Blur
single is better because it's summer and it's a good sing-a-long. It seems
that Oasis have forced the issue but they probably don't care because
they've already had a Number One. This is where people are going to
put their cards on the table. They will go for one or the other. It's kind
of like declaring undying love for one or the other. **Radio 1 *Evening
Session* presenter Jo Whiley**

I don't suppose I should say anything but I reckon Oasis will be
Number One 'cos they're more popular aren't they? I hope it's Blur,
though, 'cos they're my old boys. My new boys are Supergrass. I'm
trying to grow my sideburns but I can't, so I'll have to get some
stick-ons. **Actor and 'Parklife' vocalist Phil Daniels**

I think it's good fun and it's good for British music. It's exciting for
everybody but it's quite nerve-wracking for us. I'm quietly confident.
Somebody asked if I had money to put on one or the other, which
would I back? I'd have to say us because, if you look at the albums
we've sold, we're in good form. If the bands had released singles in

different weeks then we'd both have had more chance of getting to
Number One and in that way it would have made sense. But who
said music was about making sense? I just think the whole thing is
good fun. **Blur manager Chris Morrison**

What do I think about them releasing a single on the same date?
Not a lot, really. Oasis bring out a single every three months regardless
of anyone else. When the records are ready, we put them out. Oasis
have a superb fan base and 'Roll With It' is a great song. If the fans buy
the single, then brilliant. Noel wants to have his four Number Ones
and you can put your cards on that happening. But this band is about
the music. It's not about chart positions, it's bigger than that. But I
wouldn't bet on either song. I don't need to bet, I manage Oasis.
Oasis manager Marcus Russell

From what I can gather, Oasis have done this deliberately to set
up this competition. We started the Blur album a long way before
they started theirs. It will be a double goal for whoever gets to Number
One. There will be the getting to Number One plus the getting one
over the other band. I do think the Blur song is better. Oasis are a good
band but I don't think 'Roll With It' is up to par, so I think the whole
thing may backfire on them. Oasis are trying to stop Blur getting a
Number One single but if there's any justice in the world they won't.
They brought forward their single and it's complete shit to say we've
engineered this. If Owen Morris thinks so, he's talking out of his arse.
It's a Beatles and Stones-type situation. Fans of both bands will be
doing battle that week. **Stephen Street, producer of 'Parklife' and
'The Great Escape'**

I really don't like the Blur single but then I don't like Blur. They're a joke band. They're not even Cockneys! **Oasis producer Owen Morris**

The Blur album was scheduled for a mid-September release. That was lurching towards its inevitable release months and months ago. So with the single you can go either three or four weeks before the album. Oasis rather caught us by surprise with their single release date. We could have gone a week after that but we wouldn't. The Blur camp felt a little uncomfortable with coming out a week after. It would have looked like we were ducking out. But the over-riding concern for us is the album. There's no point in fannying about, you just have to put the boot in. **Food Records' Andy Ross**

It's great that they're both going for Number One. It's probably 30 years since it's happened. I think The Beatles and the Stones analogy is right, as long as Blur are the Beatles because I've always preferred The Beatles. I've got no idea who will win, I think it'll come down to who has the strongest record company. It's Sony versus EMI. I've heard some of the rumours about who has done what but I'm sure you can guess which side of the story I've heard.
Elastica's Justine Frischmann

That Damon is really competitive, he should just do his own thing and get on with it. **Supergrass' Gaz Coombes**

It's a big daft. It's the clash of the big guitar players. I find it quite funny that they have this level of competitiveness. I don't know how it will go. I think Oasis are really quite serious about it but I'm sure there's enough people to buy both singles. They both have enormous fan bases. I hear both their names being shouted by students in pubs. It's like a pop soap opera. **Portishead's Geoff Barrow**

I've got a tenner on Blur. The thing that's really cool is the way that they've caught everyone's attention. These bands are taking over the charts and maybe a few years ago that wouldn't have happened. They are responsible for opening the whole thing up to other bands. Everyone is crossing over, not so long ago they'd have been stuck in indie clubs with nobody paying attention but now they're in the Top 10. And I think the whole thing will get strong next year.
Sleeper singer Louise Wener

Great... I heard just before I went off to play football. Andy Ross came down to the pub to tell us. I still can't really believe it. It's been completely mad this week... every newspaper you open, there we are. I didn't think it was that big a story. It just seems really strange. But then again I suppose it is the silly season.
   Did I expect to win? To be honest, no. I sort of believed all the

papers, including *NME* who told me that Oasis were going to win. Including Phil Daniels, although he told me that was a misquote, which I can well believe. It has come as a bit of a surprise to me. **Damon when he got the news**

When the whole thing started with them, it was quite fun. It had a curiosity value, and a novelty to it. Prior to the whole thing, we got on fairly well. We weren't best mates, but there was the sense that things were going great for both bands, and that that was generally a good thing. Now, the whole war of words has left me feeling a bit saddened. It's not what I wanted to be the outcome of the 'battle of the bands' It just got so ugly. And to say things like that doesn't reflect well on them. I think they should re-assess their priorities. They'll look back on it when they're grown men and just think what dickheads they were. **Damon on Oasis's Aids-related quotes 1995**

musicians only

We've always wanted to be stars. That's what made us pick up our instruments. **Damon 1991**

I did all my grades on piano, but I write all my songs on acoustic guitar, which I can just about play ten chords on. I do them all on an E shape, and put a finger on the bottom E, so I've always got a E and B drone, whatever chord I do. That's all I do. I've limited myself massively, so the whole thing has become incredibly simple. The songs are very uncoordinated and disparate when I present them, just basic melodies and major or minor chords demoed on a little Yamaha portastudio. **Damon 1991**

We're quite strict about being musically correct, using the right chords. **Graham 1991**

My bass lines always seem more complicated when I try to simplify them. They're at their best when they're still in my head. They're absolutely perfect then. **Alex 1991**

Musically we are very good. Very good. Graham and Dave are excellent musicians, I'm pretty good and Alex isn't really that good but he's getting better all the time… **Damon 1994**

Did you know there are no bass players in *Debrett's* guide to famous people? **Alex 1991**

Us three were as good as classically trained, so that puts Alex at a bit of a disadvantage, as we have that experience of sitting in orchestras and being shouted at and Alex doesn't. **Damon 1994**

Making new music with ourselves is the most rewarding thing, the most fun thing, and the most difficult. **Graham 1991**

Remixes are like giving your dog to someone to take for a walk, and when they bring it back it's a different dog. **Alex**

I play a Gibson Les Paul guitar live because it's reliable, powerful, strong enough, and heavy enough to work really well and survive. **Graham 1991**

My bass is a white one. I don't really give a shit what instrument I play. All basses sound the same, so I don't really care. **Alex 1991**

Most of our new stuff is sung through a megaphone. I love it – it makes
me feel like a broadcaster, like Alistair Burnett. I've also got a Hohner
Melodica, and a Sixties pianola clavinet which has broken down, and
French turn-of-the-century harmonium which we used on 'Bad Day',
but that's broken down as well. And we've got an Ensoniq sampler,
which I have to use because everything else is broken. I've got quite
a lot of different instruments, but I tend to smash them up on stage –
megaphones as well. **Damon 1991**

writing & recording

We've never taken a break between albums. Two weeks off seems like a long time to us, we just want to get back to work. **Damon 1995**

When we finish one album, we immediately start thinking of the next one. **Graham 1995**

We've always seen ourselves as putting on white coats and going into the lab. **Damon 1995**

It's not me saying, 'This is how it's going to be guys'. I finish writing the songs, and then Graham takes over and makes them Psychedelic. **Damon 1990**

I have to say that I find it easy to write a great hook. Sometimes I'll write something and say to myself, 'It shouldn't be this easy'. I don't know, the songs just come out. **Damon 1995**

It wastes so much time doing it on the computer, just sitting pressing a button going, 'oh fuck, oh fuck, oh fuck,' for an hour. Sends you barmy. It's better to be able to play it yourself. **Damon 1991**

I didn't want to be an Ian Curtis. But that doesn't mean the lyric's not important. **Damon 1991**

I don't use very much vibrato. **Graham 1991**

I don't think a fourth single from any album is a good idea for anyone – no matter how good you are. **Damon 1995**

records

she's so high (their debut single, 1990)

Our idea of a 12-inch is playing ten minutes of a song and packing loads of ideas into it. Obviously the music is paramount. We have no intention of duplicating our live sound. The record should be something great, while live is more of an exhilarating thing. There's gonna be more mileage on the record. Live we can't play more than four instruments at a time, but here we're able to overdub and get a brilliant sound. It's just nice that we've gained all this experience playing around without having done a record. **Damon 1990**

leisure (1991)

We're not looking for someone to give us a sound, we just want an invisible touch, someone who'll know what we mean. The two biggest changes a producer made – one was in 'There's No Other Way'. We only had a break between the chorus and the verse once in our original song, and Stephen Street and Dave Balfe (from Food) both told us to put it in after every single chorus. The other big production thing was to speed 'Wear Me Down' up from half speed to double speed. And it still sounds slow. They're the major production points of 'Leisure'. Apart from that, the rest of the production was just getting the right sounds. **Alex 1991**

For the backwards guitar in 'Sing' I sat down and worked the whole song out backwards, turned the tape over and played it live. It's a fucking complicated way. We're very organic about that though. I won't have things sampled, then they flip it on the computer – I much prefer to do it live. **Graham 1991**

The next album will be the start of a new era. This one's been the death of the blank, directionless era we've just been though. This one is the kill Baggy album. Well, we've done that now. We've killed Baggy. Now we can concentrate on things like 'Sing' and 'Wear Me Down'. I think the true heart of Blur lies in that… noisy, emotional mess. **Damon 1991**

there's no other way (on 'leisure', 1991)

It's a much stronger vision of what we think it's all about. It's got a hook that will grind itself into people's heads and then they'll come to

see us and be utterly confused that they've heard this great pop song
and been suddenly confronted with this horrendous sort of…

That's what motivates me. Getting into people's homes, freaking
them out. It's brilliant you know. We just can't BELIEVE how easy
it is to get into the charts. **Damon 1991**

The chart position was a surprise yeah. But we knew if we got on *Top
Of The Pops* it's probable we'd go Top 10 because we had something
fresh to offer. That was OK, but when we didn't get *TOTP* the next
time, we thought fuck it. But we went up another two places. It sold
over 150,000 which is quite a lot at the moment. **Damon 1991**

bang (on 'leisure', 1991)

Although 'There's No Other Way' wasn't one of the noisiest
records, we are one of the noisiest bands in the Top 10. 'Bang' is
noisier – there's a lot more in it… I'm happier with it as a record.
Damon 1991

repetition (on 'leisure', 1991)

We're a very post-modern thing. There's a line in 'Repetition',
"Try try try, all things remain the same, so why try again?", adapted
from Beckett. I sensed that one Christmas morning when I was 18
being chased across my old school field by my old girlfriend's irate
father. I was drunk and had wanted to tell her I loved her. There's an
enormous emotional reason behind that song, but does the world give
a fuck? At the end of the day not only do we write great songs, but we
have a natural strangeness about us that makes us interesting.
Damon 1991

sing (on 'leisure', 1991)

Even people who hated us would come rushing up and say,
'What was that song?' **Graham 1995**

bad day (on 'leisure', 1991)

There are three things going on in there. Trying to write a good tune.
Trying to sound like The Beatles on one hand. And My Bloody
Valentine on the other. **Damon 1995**

popscene (single, 1992)

I'd love 'Popscene' to be a big hit. It'd be great. But then again there's

a noisy indie group on *Top Of The Pops* every week now. All looking very satisfied with their Number 18. **Damon 1992**

modern life is rubbish (1993)

You can talk to someone in a World Of Leather showroom and say 'Modern life is rubbish', and they'll go, 'Ooh I agree, it is'. It's a universal statement. **Damon 1993**

I think this is one of the most modern albums you're every going to hear. **Damon 1993**

'It was horrible trying to cram the tracks on… it could have been an 18-track album.' **Graham**

'Modern Life' was the beginning of us having an idea of what we really wanted to do. If we hadn't lost all our money we wouldn't have made two albums in a year, but it's worked. We're in control now. And 'Modern Life' was us asserting our thing of wanting to be colourful and credible, a record that'd tell numerous stories instead of one. **Damon 1994**

Modern life is the rubbish of the past. Rubbish in the sense of
a collection of debris from the past. We all live on the rubbish; it
dictates our thoughts. And because it's all built up over such a long
time, there's no necessity for originality anymore. There are so many
old things to splice together in infinite permutations that there is
absolutely no need to create anything new. I think that phrase is the
most significant comment on popular culture since 'Anarchy In
The UK'. That's why I want to graffiti it everywhere. I think it
expresses everything. **Damon 1993**

We wanted to write something like an Essex version of Dylan
Thomas' *Under Milk Wood*. Something with a very definite sense of
place, populated by very definite characters, and which would try to
encapsulate modern England – on the one had a romantic image,
and on the other faintly sinister. **Damon 1993**

villa rosie (on 'modern life is rubbish', 1993)

The bass at the intro is played with a bottleneck to produce a fucked-
up sound. Goodness knows why. Perhaps we were pretty fucked-up
at the time. **Alex 1995**

turn it up (on 'modern life is rubbish', 1993)

When we wrote it, it seemed like a good jangly pop song. But it turned out to be an MOR rock song. It didn't have any peculiarities. So we were turned off by it. **Graham 1995**

It's crap. I wouldn't have had it on the album. Balfe thought it was the only song that had a vague chance of doing well in America, so he insisted on it being there. **Damon 1995**

'Young And Lovely' (B-side of 'Chemical World') should have been on the LP. But it didn't get on there and fucking 'Turn It Up' did. **Damon**

for tomorrow (on 'modern life is rubbish', 1993)

'Everyone, wherever they are in the world knows what la la la means.' **Damon on its refrain**

sunday sunday (on 'modern life is rubbish', 1993)

I decided that 'modern life was rubbish' one Sunday afternoon in America. I wrote a song called 'Sunday Sunday' which, on the surface, seems like a grand nostalgic romp, but it's not. It was about the scary feeling I got looking out of a Minneapolis hotel room onto ye olde, make-believe plastic country square they'd constructed in the middle of this giant shopping mall. That view brought into my head all this imagery and emotion. I realised 'I don't wanna be in America, I wanna be where I come from. Get me home!' Funnily enough, the band all felt the same way. **Damon 1995**

parklife (1994)

'Parklife' is a more radioscopic album than 'Modern Life'. It's a trip through the radio bands, each song from a different station. 'Modern Life' was a daytime record, full of colourful Persil adverts. 'Parklife' is more nocturnal – it's porn and cable TV and misfits. **Damon 1994**

With 'Modern Life Is Rubbish' the characters weren't so nocturnal. They lived in the day, and didn't get up to anything naughty. But on this album they start out in the daylight and quickly descend into the darker regions of themselves. **Damon 1994**

I do think we've got a lot better. I doubt if you can genuinely say you've heard an album that sounds like 'Parklife' before, because I don't think you have. **Damon 1994**

There's no longer the clear agenda where if you work really hard and get your exams, you'll get a job, you'll get a wife, you'll get a life. There's such an abyss between what you should do and what actually happens. Most 12-13 year old kids in inner cities fuck their brains up on Butane before they get a chance to do well in their exams. Man is going from one state to another. We're going through a very fine sieve. And that's probably why our album 'Parklife' is so eclectic. Maybe it's on the other side of the sieve. **Damon 1994**

On 'Leisure' the lyrics were deliberately non-political, completely, but that's not going to be the case for the next album. They will be apolitical, but they won't be as blank. Beforehand, it was singing songs about waking up in the morning, having a cup of coffee, getting in a taxi, having a couple of drinks, hitting my head against a wall and going home. Now, it's getting up in the morning, looking in the mirror, picking a spot, feeling I've got a bit of a toothache, sore throat, hair's falling out, getting in a taxi and realising I haven't got enough money, and my heartbeat's increasing, getting stuck in traffic, getting out, having a couple of drinks… Lyrically it's much more urban, less generalised. And musically, we know the way the music is going – it's a lot more um, urban. **Damon 1991**

Sophisticated. We're becoming more interested in not being complacent about sounds. There'll be unconventional guitar sounds – in every song it won't just be fuzzy strumming guitars. **Graham 1991**

The thing about this album is that in a lot of ways it's a massive departure from the last one. If people are scared of that, there's not much I can do about it. I just can't think of anything more boring than doing the same thing over and over again. **Damon 1994**

The diversity of 'Parklife' was exactly what we're trying to achieve. For me the album is like a loosely linked concept involving all these different stories. It's the travels of the mystical lager-eater, seeing what's going on in the world and commenting on it. It's the same idea as the poem *Confessions Of An Opium Eater*, but that sounds much too sensitive. Everyone goes on about the ideal of the sensitive artist, but for me that's all bollocks, I can't stand the idea of being a sad, lonely bedsit poet. I'd much rather be perceived as loud and arrogant, because all our sensitivity's in our records. **Damon 1994**

When you get past platinum you know it's a classic of its generation. The record company want it to sell 500,000, and it will. There hasn't been a sale like this since The Jam. Not even The Smiths sold this many. **Damon 1994**

I create these characters but I can't really be them. It's too difficult. **Damon on his attempt to narrate the Cockney vocal**

'Parklife' became a word as opposed to an album. It was actually a 'way of being'. **Damon 1995**

On the Japanese version of the 'Parklife' CD, the dog's eyes light and when you open it... it BARKS! **Graham 1994**

girls and boys (on 'parklife', 1994)

It's about the meat markets there. It's not a dig at those sort of 18-30 people, more a celebration. That soft-porn feel runs throughout the whole album. **Damon 1994**

Yeah, it's about those sorts of holidays. I went on holiday with Justine last summer to Magaluf and the place was just equally divided between cafes serving up full English breakfast and really tacky Essex nightclubs. There's a very strong sexuality about it. I just love the whole idea of it, to be honest. I love herds. All these blokes and all these girls meeting at the watering hole and then just... copulating. There's no morality involved. I'm not saying it should or shouldn't happen. My mind's just getting more dirty. I can't help it.
Damon 1994

The Pet Shop Boys have agreed to do a mix of it for us, and that should be brilliant. What I'm hoping for is that they can come up with a version that becomes the big summer hit in all those nightclubs in Spain and Majorca. That's exactly what we want. I'd love those people to be into Blur... **Damon 1994**

london loves (on 'parklife', 1994)

'London Loves' is about a character in a car driving out and fucking up, basically. I like to chart a character's story from A to B. However microscopic their environment, they do travel, and suffer some sort of psychosis in that journey. **Damon 1994**

tracy jacks (on 'parklife', 1994)

They fascinate me, all those dead seaside towns on the East coast, Walton On The Naze, Frinton. They have one guesthouse and it's boarded up. It's a couple of council estates, a few old houses and the bleak, bleak North Sea. They're half-places.
  'Tracy Jacks' is about a city gent who leaves his house, gets on a train, goes to a seaside town, takes his clothes off and gets arrested, then goes home and bulldozes his house. **Damon 1994**

magic america (on 'parklife', 1994)

It's not paranoid. It's just that I feel physically unwell when I'm in America. I can't help that I have this Americaphobia. I don't want us to come across as these venomous, anti-American Brits. I find it difficult to adapt to the scale of America. America eats us up. I had to write that one seething little song and get it out of my system. It's more subtle than you think. I used phrases from adverts for the lyrics, and musically it's quite cartoon-like. It's a song which could serenade you through a shopping centre. I don't think we'll do it again. **Damon 1994**

end of a century (on 'parklife', 1994)

It's about how couples get into staying in and staring at each other. Only instead of candle-light, it's the TV light. **Damon**

this is a low (on 'parklife', 1994)

It's about people taking smack. **Alex**

I thought it was a gouched-out song. **Graham**

We always found the shipping forecast soothing. We used to listen to it in America to remind us of home. It's very good for a hangover. Good cure for insomnia, too. **Alex**

I'd had this line – "And into the sea go pretty England and me for a long time. So I started at the Bay of Biscay. Back for tea". 'Tea' rhymes with 'me'. And then I went "Hit traffic on the Dogger Bank". 'Bank' – 'rank' – so up the Thames to find a taxi rank. And I just went round. **Damon**

bank holiday (on 'parklife', 1994)

The first time we recorded it was a Radio One session for Mark Goodier (in July 1993). We hadn't really written it properly. **Graham**

the great escape (1995)

The title 'The Great Escape' is about the fact that I think there's very few people on this planet who don't think about escaping something that is going on in their lives every five minutes – everybody's escaping. And it's extraordinary the lengths to which we all go to try and escape.

I knew I'd be close to the characters in it and I'd be singing more about my own dilemmas through other people than I have before. I'd have less distance from the whole thing than before. It would be more intimate… I just feel I've grown up a bit. I feel more adult now. And as such, I think we've made an adult album. It's quite natural really, we've had a rather extended adolescence, which ended last year. **Damon 1995**

Everything is going to be darker on this album. Full stop. **Damon 1995**

It's not a concept album, but our last two albums have had a common thread. All the songs have been about some condition, some society, whether it be paranoia or… anything. This one seems to be about corruption and Prozac. **Graham 1995**

The album's definitely sadder. We've got a lot of songs in the vein of 'This Is A Low', which is one of the best things I've ever done. But there's also the punkiest song we've ever done, much more punk than 'Bank Holiday'. We felt we'd produced an album of extremes with 'Parklife', but this is going to have more extremes. **Damon 1995**

I'd like to think there are at least two songs on this album that MTV would go for. With a cracking video and a bit of touring, it could happen for them. **Producer Stephen Street 1995**

Every single song is as good as the best one on 'Parklife'. It's a wealth of riches. 'Parklife' was a fairly British album, but the new stuff is more universal. **Food boss Andy Ross 1995**

It is a step on from 'Parklife', but it won't alienate anybody who got into Blur with it. It's a bit darker, but I think that was the only way for us to go. **Producer Stephen Street 1995**

It's definitely the best thing we've ever done. Although it was weird to make, because it was all done at the time when the attention was on us for 'Parklife'. 'Parklife' was in the Top 10 every single week when we were recording this one, so we had to keep switching our attention between the two. **Damon 1995**

It's quite a doom-laden album in areas. But it's like, we're serious about the humour. Serious about being funny. I don't blame them for it, but people do listen pretty straight-faced to our music when they first hear it. There's a kind of sinister-ness to it, which is meant to be funny, a lot of it. **Graham 1995**

The more I listen to what I've written for the next set of recordings, the more I think that a lot of the chirpy, Cockney side of it was just a

lack of confidence about the more emotional side of what we're about.
I'm becoming less chirpier about life in general. I'm becoming a
morose git. **Damon 1995**

country house (on 'the great escape', 1995)

The new single is, I'll admit, a catchy pop song, but why should that
be something to be ashamed of? **Damon**

You think it's a bit Madness and a bit Beatles? Maybe you're right.
There's certainly something in it that pulls you in. There's two things
going on at the same time. It sounds really simple, but it's not the sort
of thing that anyone could do. Blur songs aren't as straightforward
as everyone thinks. **Graham**

yuko and hiro (on 'the great escape', 1995)

The Japanese audience loved it. It's a big thing here, that song.
My preoccupation with people in suits going mad is part of the culture

here. One of the big things the businessmen do here is to take their ties off and tie them round their heads as headbands when they're really drunk. It's some sort of symbolic thing. I did that before 'Yuko And Hiro' last night, and the crowd went bananas. **Damon 1995**

the universal (on 'the great escape', 1995)

We've written one called 'The Universal' which is very Burt Bacharach. It's almost a wall of sound, but not a guitar wall of sound. **Damon 1995**

When we were finishing off the album, the National Lottery was the big thing. The advertising around it – that ghostly, godlike hand pointing at you, and that assumption of immediate happiness… You can't help alluding to things that are around at the time you're writing. Otherwise, you're not doing your job. It would have been the second single, but I like the idea of it as a Christmas single because it's not at all uplifting. It is probably a more realistic option for Christmas. **Damon 1995**

oliver's army
(a cover version of elvis costello's 1979 hit recorded for 'peace together' in 1993 to promote peace in northern ireland)

What's the point in trying to improve on something you already like? Plus you only get half the money. **Alex**

It's a disaster – one of the worst things we've done. **Damon**

es schmecht (b side of 'chemical world' 12-inch)

It's the most low-tech thing we've ever done, but I liked it. It's a strange, Can-influenced piece. **Damon**

supa shoppa (b side of 'parklife')

You don't fuck about with a real flautist on a B-side. **Alex on the synthesised flutes**

beard (b side of 'parklife' 12-inch)

Total cod jazz. Chromatic scales with notes dropped at random. **Alex**

We could have called it 'Pipe' or 'Beret'. **Graham**

on stage

Just look at the world we live in. For God's sake, it's completely mad. And I think it needs people to be on stage and be a little bit mad and… Theatrical's a really bad word for it but, yeah, we are a little bit of theatre. **Damon 1991**

It was actually the first time we'd ever played the Dublin Castle. We'd done the Falcon a lot, but never there. It was too small to do anything but play the really punky songs and probably because it was so different from Mile End it made it so brilliant. I had a great time. We all did. **Graham on secret pub gig 1995**

The Milton Keynes gig with REM is important. It's completely different from the Mile End gig, but it's a step forward for us. And a challenge. There's people who've come to see us, but loads more who've only turned up to see REM We're going to make them like us too. **Damon 1995**

Playing at Glastonbury on a lovely summer evening as the sun set was quite unbeatable really. **Damon 1995**

I like things to repulse people, to upset and move them. I don't want to give people an identity, I want to give them a crisis. **Damon**

Our new show will be more theatrical. We've got this giant Prozac pill that comes down for 'The Universal' and splits open. **Damon 1995**

I'm a bit embarrassed by it really. But I just feel like doing it. It's not very ordered. I'd like to be able to dance properly, but jumping around like a lunatic is the only thing I can do with any feeling. These days I steer clear of Graham 'cos I'm terrified of him killing me. Alex just pushes me off the stage. One gig we did, I jumped up on his shoulders, the stage was just about four feet high and he just decided to jump. It was like a double stagedive with bass guitar, everyone got out of the way… and I got quite badly damaged. **Damon 1990**

We're not a mad, irresponsible band. Our gigs don't usually end up in a blood-bath.
   A lot of the venues have got really pissed off with us, like really emotional about it all, saying, 'We have much bigger bands that you playing here all the time and none of them behave like you!' That just shows how staid it all is if it's such a shock to see someone doing things like that. **Damon 1990**

When we first started, from the time we went on stage till the time
we left, I was just like a human whirlwind, just everywhere, not
singing properly, just being really crap. I jumped off everything and
careered into anything and everybody and I just didn't care. I thought
it was great to have a bloody nose and be sick and everything. And we
started getting people shouting between songs, 'Hurt yourself! Jump
off the PA! Fucking kick me! *Be sick!! Be sick!*' It became a cliché really
quickly so we started to think about it more.

Now because people have got this expectation of us being totally
mad, and because we only do it when it feels totally right, we must
disappoint some people, especially on those nights when we're really
happy just to play the songs. **Damon 1991**

People could say we deliberately have the stage presence we have to
wind people up or deliberately write songs which are slightly quirky to
wind people up. It's not like that at all. It's just what we are. It's just us.
That image actually appeals to us as people. **Damon 1991**

The Reading Festival (1993) was amazing. It was the first time that
I was ever in control of my performance. It was a lovely feeling having
the audience singing along. And I suddenly realised what we were,
I discovered the key – that sort of call and response reaction, the
electric quality of gathering lots of different kinds of people together.

I mean, we played Norwich the other night and there were
15-18 year olds at the front and, at the back, there were men with
beards – and great beards at that! And they were all singing. And that's
the way I've always seen it. You see, I wasn't particularly into the
rebellion thing when I was a teenager. I didn't read the *NME* and
get into all that one-upmanship. I've always thought that music is
there for everybody. **Damon 1994**

When you're on stage, it's such a rush when everything's going
properly. Like we played at Brixton just before Christmas and for me
it was just like a big orgasm all the way through the show. So how can
you sit still through that? You'd just explode wouldn't you?
Dave 1991

The more you perform on stage, the more you can't help but
develop a bit of artistry to it. Iggy Pop, Julian Cope, Jagger, they all
had it. The more you do it, the more you start to learn the barriers of
it and the doors it has for you. I didn't sit down and think, 'Right,
I'm going to do that onstage', but now I do it onstage I start to think
about the possibilities. An idea I had which I'd like to develop was a
kind of pushing the limits of physical theatre to a point where people
didn't know if it was real or if it was theatre. I'd say ten per cent is
still theatre. **Damon 1990**

all around the world

It'll be called the Rollercoaster tour, and will have some very big names, and we'll be playing places like G-MEX and Wembley Arena. They'll all be good bands, and everyone's going to change places in the running order every night, like Siouxsie & The Banshees' American Lollapalooza tour. It will be the first time that anything like that has happened in Britain in 20 years. **Damon on summer '92 tour 1991**

We're playing all over the place in December, to 180,000 people. We're doing some arenas, but one thing we won't be doing is playing Wembley Stadium. That's where I draw the line. We'll be doing some open-air shows (next year), but they'll be more like festival things that we're setting up ourselves. I can't be too specific, but we just want to do something that's about music. **Damon 1995**

Will Blur become successful in the USA? I'm not entirely sure what we do will translate well on MTV, because it's geared to that sort of juvenile thing. I think that's our fundamental dilemma in becoming a bigger band. We can do it to a degree in Europe, because Europe is much more tangible – we can still reach the press and reach the fans through touring. But I still have this wonderful dream that American kids will start to get it and actually understand what we're all about. **Damon 1995**

We were approaching Madrid airport on an Iberia flight from Barcelona when our tour manager, who was sitting next to me, grabbed hold of my left leg. I said, 'Fuck off Ian,' but he wouldn't let go so I hit him. I then looked at the other passengers and noticed they had the same look of complete panic on their faces as he did. I asked him what was wrong and he said, 'We nearly died.'
   Apparently, the plane had approached the runway almost on its side with the left wing no more than six feet off the ground. Just before impact, the pilot had managed to right the plane so avoiding disaster and probably our death. For the rest of the day everyone got completely drunk and told all and sundry how much they loved them. I felt strangely distant as I had not shared the experience. **Damon**

I just started to miss really simple things (while touring America). I missed people queuing up in shops. I missed people saying 'goodnight' and the BBC. I missed having 15 minutes between commercial breaks. And I missed people having respect for my geographical roots, because Americans don't care if you're from Inverness or Land's End. I missed everything about England. **Damon**

I've been to an American Football game in San Francisco, the

Oakland Raiders, and I realised a lot of stuff about American culture that I hadn't realised before. The way the whole thing is geared towards constant gratification. They like their pleasure highly organised. **Damon 1995**

The problem with Germans…' no offence or anything but they're all Damon – they all want to be in charge! **Alex**

There's a point where you start losing the intimacy of what you do, and I'm not prepared to get into the thing where because we played this size of venue this year, we've got to play somewhere twice the size next year. It doesn't lead anywhere. You just end up playing the wrong gigs with Tina Turner and Bryan Adams. That's not why we wanted to become a big band. We wanted to do something that meant something, rather than just saying, 'We're the biggest band in the world.' Wembley Stadium is for wankers. **Damon 1995**

Big places are where we have to play, but they're not necessarily where we want to spend all our time. This tour will be fun.
Damon on 1995 summer tour

It vaguely annoys me that people say we've never done anything in America when we went four months touring there with 'Leisure'. We've gone there every year, we sell out 3,000 seater venues across the country and 'Girls And Boys' went Top 50 there. How many other British bands do that? I think we actually are a failure in America. We should be selling five million there to be comparatively successful. From our point of view, we should be the ones doing the best out there because we've been around the longest and are, as far as we're concerned, the best. But life isn't like that. **Damon 1995**

They have a very positive attitude about America now. They've had some bad experiences in the past, but they're ready for it now. We live in hope. **Parlophone MD Tony Wadsworth 1995**

You have to like Japan, a place where you can get described as 'handsome and atmospheric'. They're so well-informed but I don't know if they actually like us. Well, on one level, they do to a ridiculous degree. They like the West so much they're willing to change their physical appearance for us. **Damon 1991**

There's always such an undercurrent of repression in Japan. They've got very strict rules. At the Budokan you're not allowed to smoke onstage, and there's a 10 foot drop from the stage down to audience level, then 20 foot to the audience, so there's absolutely no opportunity for the audience to get near you or you to get to them. But I went over that and ran into the audience and caused chaos on

two occasions, and was actually banned from playing there ever
again for about half an hour. I'm now only allowed to play there if
I promise never to do it again.

I hate not being allowed to have any contact. I like to clown about
a bit. When we started, I liked to climb about all over the place, but
as we go on it gets harder. The speaker stacks keep getting higher
and higher. **Damon 1995**

It went pretty well in America… we're a cult band. A few years ago
we'd have thought we were doing really well, but, of course, now
we're playing big places everywhere else. In America, we're playing
places like the Palace in LA and the Academy in New York, which
are about 2,000 capacity. You can have false starts that look like you're
doing really well, but then you go back and nobody's interested.
Damon 1995

American 'alternative mainstream' at the moment has arrived at a
point of crisis. It's reverted to type. It did have a period where there
was some kind of agenda, and you did get a sense that bands were
playing because they felt something big inside themselves. But Nirvana
and The Beastie Boys were the only examples of that kind of thing as a
real voice, although there were other players. It's not happening over
there at the moment, and, in a way, that makes it harder for us, because
what is selling and what is popular is really bland. You'd have thought
that if there's a downturn in the quality of American music, then it's
better for British bands. But it's not as simple as that. **Damon 1995**

The Japanese seem very insular, very self-contained. Like the way
they mob us at the hotel. It's in your face but they don't say anything.
It's very serene. **Alex 1991**

We have got a fanatical fan base in America. When we were in
Los Angeles, this guy showed us his Lambretta with all of the names
of our songs painted on it. It was amazing. But they're Anglophiles,
it's hard to assess it all really, because you're talking about obsessive
people. **Damon**

Detroit is the end of the world. Maybe we should do a cover of
'Ghost Town' tonight. It's the perfect place for it. **Damon**

You want to know about Blur in America? Well, this is the sixth time
we've been here. So we're fairly realistic about the whole thing, we've
learnt you've got to be nice. **Damon**

Union Jacks were the only flags we've seen at one of our shows so far.
But you get your ex-pats and all your British people who are working
over here, and I suppose coming to see us play is sort of cosy. If I was

here I'd go to see a British band, no matter who they were. **Damon**

In Detroit it was a bit odd. Most of the fans looked like extras from
Blow-Up, but tonight they were slightly more sophisticated, I thought.
The main thing, having been here so many times, is that this is the first
time they're prepared to get into the whole campiness of it all. The sort
of flippant… we mean this but we don't really mean this – but fuck
you if you think we mean this, 'cos we don't mean it because we
mean it. **Damon**

The great thing about America is, it takes at least five years for
anything to wear off. It's ultra hip to be into Britpop, which is funny.
Anyway, you can't cash in on anything in America, you have to work
for it, and we've worked our asses off. We may have opened the door
for everybody in Britain, but we're only concerned about our own
minute slice of the cake. **Damon**

I think they like our accents, but in America, you do have to give
that sense that you're rockin! It does pose problems for us because,
whenever that conversation comes up, I always say we're a pop band.
We don't rock. It's a point of principle. **Damon 1995**

You'd have thought it was Wolverhampton or somewhere.
They were well up for it. They smelt of rollmops and sugar.
Damon 1995 on Copenhagen

Touring's a dream. You don't have to pay for anything, you go to a
different place every day, everywhere you go you get beer and drugs
free, girls scream at you and you feel… shit actually. most of the time.
But it's good. **Alex 1990**

No, no, it's just fun, isn't it? It's just a big, huge novelty. Everywhere
we go is packed out and that's brilliant because we've had to struggle
with 20 or 30 people in the audience, trying to get them going.
And now, immediately you get onstage, there's that excitement
and you play a lot better and you actually start to love it. **Damon 1990**

America made us realise what a wonderfully quiet, undramatic place
Britain is. We wrote virtually all the songs while we were out there.
And when we came back we realised how much we like being British.
The trouble is, when you start giving out those signals everyone thinks
you're a fascist. You are not allowed to be British. You are not allowed
to be German. But you are, of course, always allowed to be American.
Alex

Life for many Americans exists within these huge sheds, and you can
eat and buy your shoes, listen to music and buy your health insurance.

Almost go to the hospital. Jog. In these huge bubbles. And that really made us look at England and see how much of the American culture had been absorbed into a very innocent England. The Americans do it with an immense sort of panache – they are lobotomised, sanitised automatons – but they do it with such panache that you view it as a trait of being American. Whereas in England it makes me sick. **Damon 1993**

videos & image

You can't underestimate the importance of long legs and a good haircut in this business. **Alex 1991**

The video for 'There's No Other Way' is about people who buy possessions which have no life to them. It's about people creating a completely lifeless world around them but being convinced it's the right thing because they've spent all this money. This family just let us do it. They were really thrilled we borrowed their house. They didn't realise that we were going in there and just burying them in their own lives. I know a lot of people will miss the point, they'll think, 'What is this? It's nothing'. But those sorts of people will never get it. That's the joke.

It should make you feel great, great that you're not like that. And when our video gets shown on *Top Of The Pops*, there's gonna be millions of people watching it and it's gonna be like a mirror into their homes, into their lives. It will be like we've got a camera looking at them. That amuses me. **Damon 1991**

I hate the video for 'Country House'. I love the song but the association with it has become Page Three and Benny Hill instead of Blur. **Graham 1995**

Because 'Country House' has that sort of video, immediately the song is judged in that way. I think we did the wrong kind of video. I can't hold my hands on my heart and say it was good art. **Damon 1995**

If you rate yourself as a performer you should be happy to let your music do the talking. **Oasis' Liam Gallagher on Blur's gimmicky video 1995**

We could look like Ride in photos but we always try not to. Something stops us being happy with that and somehow everything we do ends up being kind of confusing. And that's what we are. There's something that stops us from being a classic indie band and makes us something else. I don't know what it is though… sorry. **Damon 1991**

ambitions, direction, motivation

You know what made me want to be in a band? It was seeing a
South Bank Show on The Smiths, and hearing Morrissey say that pop
music was dead, and that The Smiths had been the last group of any
importance. I was round at Graham's house, and I remember thinking,
'No one is going to tell me that pop music is finished'. **Damon 1991**

We worked hard to be what we are and we're gonna have to work
a lot harder to be what we really wanna be, which is a band that is an
adjective as opposed to a name. **Damon 1990**

I've noticed my motivation to do more of what I want to do increase.
Selling a lot of records makes you want to be a lot better y'know, not
compromise one iota. The more successful you get the more important
it is to be yourself because you're opening yourself up to so many more
people. If you go down an avenue which isn't pure and reasoned then
you just get completely fucked up. **Damon 1991**

I've seen people who've started to sell a lot of records, and the music's
just become less important, it's just part of the machine. **Damon 1991**

What we want to do is cultivate that chemical inside you that gives
you belief in things. When we brought out 'Modern Life…' it was
different, we were on the defensive. But now we've broken through
all those preconceptions and we can really start. When we first started,
I always said to people, don't judge us, wait until five years from now.
But maybe now's the time to take over. There's just so much stuff
to get out… what's that expression? Yeah, that's what we are.
Anal expulsives! **Damon 1994**

The charts are like a street – like a cul–de–sac within a housing
estate. You have nice neighbours and horrible ones. We want to be in
Number 3 next to the newsagent. **Damon 1994**

We wanna be huge, we wanna be in the charts. Because there
are so many bands, so much music that doesn't do anything for
anyone that is huge and is in the charts that you just wanna be there.
Well I do, anyway. **Damon 1990**

I think people have just got to give us a chance to put out an album, or
a couple of albums, before they start forming opinions. I mean Blur are
a couple of singles and a couple of good live shows at the moment…

there's a lot more to come. I'd like over 10 years to be able to release an album a year and all together it will start making sense. Like the way Felt did an album every year, y'know, I don't want to produce a Felt album, but I like the idea of gradual embellishment and exploration of the band. **Damon 1991**

I really want to write music that is more universal. I see so many limitations to what we do. I've got to divorce myself from writing songs that have that semi-detached quality and go for shopping centres. This is the way I think about music and that's why people get confused about us. I want this album to reach that Britannia Book Club level. Y'know, take your trousers down at the Brits and then come back with an album that competes with Garth Brooks but is intelligent. That's the future for me. I can't see any alternative really. **Damon 1994**

We're very serious emotionally. I mean we create emotions in people – and not just good emotions – crap emotions as well. That's our strong point, emotive music… lyrically erudite. If I felt I could do more for the world by giving this up and travelling around England with a guitar and just singing, I'd do it. If I was in Central Africa, that would be a more worthwhile thing to do, but we live in such a complex society that my role as someone who entertains and lifts spirits only works on a level that is satisfied by me becoming incredibly famous and successful. The familiarity to people of what we do is important.

I feel I've got the ability to lift people's spirits and give them something…y'know, our fans at the moment send us letters saying

they're genuinely moved by some of our songs. I'm getting loads of
people coming up to me and saying 'I thought Robert Smith was
the most important person and now you are', which is all bollocks.
But if you can do that sort of thing, that's enough. **Damon 1991**

When I sing certain songs and you can see people singing along and
they're lyrics which mean something to me – the fact that they know
the words is rewarding. That's an absolute, that communication with
people, I like working towards certain absolutes… (like) just striving
for a state of being which doesn't allow unnecessary arrogance and
selfishness. I can't see the point in getting up in the morning if you're
not going to better yourself.

 I mean, I know we're not perceived as the coolest of bands…
but six months ago no-one would've been interested in coming to
our gigs and now, somehow, we're becoming sort of, what's the word,
well we're growing in stature in people's heads, purely because we're
sticking to what we were.

 Maybe our attitudes were a little ambitious six months ago but
they're more in context now. If anything I've got more humility by
just achieving that minor hurdle of having a hit. You do genuinely
believe that… I don't want to create a cerebral minefield in people's
heads like Morrissey did or Robert Smith. They used very easy
references for teenagers. It's very easy to tell a teenager who's going
through a chemical change that 'It's not worth it, oh dear, oh dear'…
it's a lot harder to get through to people that they're great – that they
should be totally into everything. I don't want to turn them into
capitalists or selfish gits… but I know from my own background,
it doesn't do anyone any harm to be told they're OK. **Damon 1991**

Pop music is my one chosen thing, it's what drives me on and I want
to be at the centre of things. **Damon 1995**

I quite like being set challenges. I like taking risks. But it's a school
thing really, isn't? When you get older, you just do things. You don't
really need someone to dare you. **Damon 1995**

I'm not afraid of failure in the wider sense, but I am intensely
annoyed about personal failure, about not doing my best work.
That is unbearable. I've got enough ego to cope with not selling
records, but if I think I'm doing shit, I can't take it. **Damon 1995**

It's easy to say this now but we find this very stimulating on a cerebral,
physical, and a very spiritual level. As soon as one of those disappears
off the equation, it's over. **Damon 1991**

I'm very sceptical about emotions. I strive towards simple emotive
expressions. I basically strive towards simplicity in everything. And it

distresses me that I can't find anyone, or anything, that's as simple as
I would wish it to be. Which is mad, because Blur are very complex.
Damon 1991

I have to be unhappy to write words. But all those bands like early
Pink Floyd and The Kinks had that in common – that resolute kind
of tragi-comic aspect that we've got. It comes from being content with
your lot – middle class, affluent, y'know, suburbia – yet feeling that
the society you live in is losing its grace, becoming squalid.

We are a generation brought up with the nuclear threat. By the
time we were able to think for ourselves, there was this inevitability
that we'd all die in a nuclear holocaust. And therefore we had to resign
ourselves that we were starting off on a doomed life, almost. And even
though my own influences as a child were overridingly positive that's
an influence that has never left us. That blank resigned feeling we had
as teenagers. That strong temptation to become incredibly passive and
recognise the futility in aimless slogans and just refuse to be anything.
Damon 1991

the future

There is a contradiction in using the past and rebelling against the future. There is a contradiction in what we are. **Damon 1994**

There's nothing more up to date and relevant that Blur. We're like The Jam, The Smiths and The Stone Roses were in place and time. Next year we'll have to recreate ourselves and we'll either be clear enough to know what's going wrong to get it right or we'll be too detached. **Damon 1991**

At the moment, all I've got are just songs on a Walkman, but we want to have a bit more anarchy in the way we record. Having worked with someone like Tricky, who goes in the studio and has no regard for convention at all, and just does things you shouldn't do, but they sound great, was quite a revelation to me. I'd like to work more with that sort of attitude. **Damon 1995**

The only thing we haven't done, which I want to try on the next album, is a really good quality muzak track, because I don't think there's enough of it. I really like the concept of muzak. It's musical medication. **Damon 1995**

I've still not really come to terms with mortality. I'm still immature about that. It's like if you get pregnant, you get happy hormones, who-gives-a-fuck? hormones, and as I get older, I hope to get some of them. **Damon 1995**

over to you...

This unsigned and unheard of Colchester band played a blinder which
swiftly endeared them to the Dingwalls disaffected. There could well
be a gap in the goofy market and Seymour have the charm to fill it.
Music Week **on Seymour, May 1989**

Alex is a dickhead of such magnitude that next to him even Gazza
seems bearable. **Unnamed Scottish journalist**

If The Stone Roses are The Beatles and Happy Mondays are
The Stones, then Blur are The Who. **Unknown journalist 1990**

Their passionate view of Brit pop looks an idea whose time has come.
The Face

When did young girls last scream at anyone this brazenly talented? *Q*

The new Blur album has two or three tracks that derive from what I've
done, but it has an added twist. I'd rather Damon ripped off something
from me than Simple Minds. **Ex-Special Terry Hall 1995**

When 'Modern Life Is Rubbish' came out I thought they were
the greatest group in the world. All Damon's references are spot-on,
and Graham is probably the maddest guitarist since (XTC's)
Andy Partridge. **Nick Heyward 1995**

The Smiths were one of the few bands who could do any kind of
song and still be instantly recognisable, and Blur are the same.
Stephen Street 1995

The corporate answer is that I wasn't expecting 'Parklife's'
success, but I'm not surprised. But of course I didn't bloody expect it.
I shouldn't say this, but we would have been happy with 200,000 sales.
That figure would have had us celebrating down the pub.
Food Records' Andy Ross 1995

The UK was struggling to make new music with any real impact
on the general public but 'Parklife' did that and has given hope and
confidence to new bands out there. Traditional UK pop guitar bands
now have more of a chance alongside all the dance and US acts.
Andy's Records owner Andy Gray 1995

There are many reasons why 'Parklife' is a great album but, basically,
it caught people's imagination with its diversity and the fact that, as a

band, they really can play. Blur's potential to reinterpret great influences has had a tremendous knock-on effect. **BBC DJ Steve Lamacq 1995**

Working with Graham Coxon, it began to dawn that I had met the best guitarist I'd worked with since Johnny Marr. I rate him as the best guitarist around. He plays things Johnny wouldn't even think of. **Producer Stephen Street 1995**

I wanted them to conquer the globe. There's more to life than just getting *New Musical Express* and *Select* covers. **Dave Balfe, owner of Food Records 1995**

It's been quite funny watching the way that the media have portrayed Brett and Damon as opposite ends of the scale: that one is the effeminate thinker and the other is the beer-drinking Essex lout when, in fact, they're remarkably similar. **Justine Frischmann, Elastica 1994**

Would I kick Damon out of bed? Yeah, I think I would. Who wants to shag that? He looks like such a sissy. I like my men with a bit of meat on 'em. **Lily Savage**

'I Go To Sleep' features a piano accompaniment by Damon. Isn't he good? He's classically-trained apparently. We thought we'd get in a piano player for maybe one or two songs, just to add a little texture to the thing, and Stephen Street suggested Damon. We ran through the song once and that was it. He's like us – no-one wants to rehearse. **Chrissie Hynde, The Pretenders**

The first band that really got me into listening to music was Blur. My favourite song's 'Tracy Jacks'. It was Oasis that made me actually want to be in a band, but if it hadn't have been for that excitement at those small Blur gigs, we'd never have felt that buzz, that thing about being part of something. **Chris Gentry, Menswear 1995**

I first saw Seymour at the Powerhaus in October '89 and, well, they were a bit crap really, but had some exceedingly good bits in between. Crap but entertaining. We weren't going to sign a band called Seymour – it's a crap name and Blur is a fine name – and that was simply part and parcel of us getting involved with them. It was just good advice. There are enough bands around with crap names. When it came to the music we could only suggest that they concentrate on the good stuff rather than the daft stuff. That's not contrived, just common sense. **Food Records' Andy Ross 1991**

They're incredibly prolific. All the great acts have gone through a period of intense creativity, like Bowie in the early RCA years and

The Smiths who produced a load of great singles as well as the albums. Blur are there now. But their great strength is they are a band. They hang out together naturally and whatever they do together works. **Producer Stephen Street 1991**

All my bands cared in their own way and had a real on-the-edge humour. It's the same with Blur, just further on. Instead of just having a few bits of the puzzle, they've got the lot. They're practically the perfect example of commerce meeting art head on – and working. **Manager Mike Collins 1991**

Damon was hunched over a mini-keyboard, plinking out an insane piece of Satie-esque doggerel, while the others built and demolished a wall of noise that caught the ear. *Sounds* **journalist Leo Finlay after a Seymour gig 1989**

Blur are not lads. Apart from Dave, who fits most neatly into the regular geezer category, arch-epicurean Alex is like a character from *Brideshead Revisited*, Graham is a hedonistic, self-destructive pretty boy while Damon reminds me of Hywel Bennett in some Technicolor mid-Sixties film, or Michael Caine in *Alfie*, half middle-class theatrical who's about to go 'Daaahling!' at any moment, and half Cockney wideboy heartbreaker. **Journalist Paul Lester 1990**